to ______________________________

from ______________________________

date ______________________________

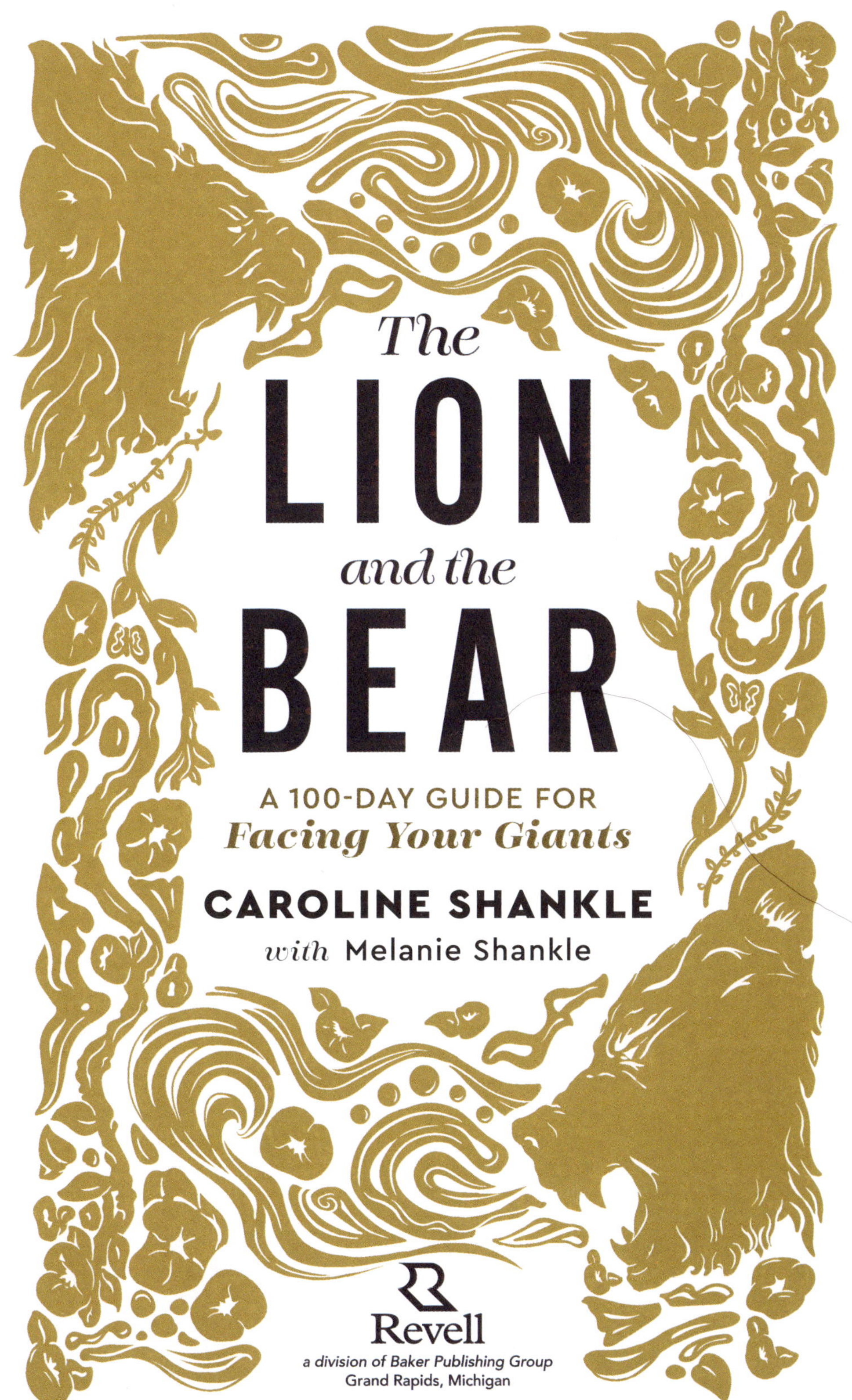

The LION and the BEAR

A 100-DAY GUIDE FOR *Facing Your Giants*

CAROLINE SHANKLE

with Melanie Shankle

Revell

a division of Baker Publishing Group

Grand Rapids, Michigan

Published by Revell
a division of Baker Publishing Group
Grand Rapids, Michigan
RevellBooks.com

Printed in Colombia

Library of Congress Cataloging-in-Publication Data
Names: Shankle, Melanie author | Shankle, Caroline author
Title: The lion and the bear : a 100-day guide for facing your giants / Melanie Shankle and Caroline Shankle.
Description: Grand Rapids, Michigan : Revell, a division of Baker Publishing Group, [2025] | Includes bibliographical references.
Identifiers: LCCN 2025000820 | ISBN 9780800746926 cloth | ISBN 9781493451067 ebook
Subjects: LCSH: Teenage girls—Prayers and devotions | Stress (Psychology)—Religious aspects—Christianity | Devotional literature
Classification: LCC BV4860 .S436 2025 | DDC 242/.62—dc23/eng/20250414
LC record available at https://lccn.loc.gov/2025000820

Cover illustration by Nate Eidenberger
Cover design by Laura Klynstra

The author is represented by Alive Literary Agency, www.aliveliterary.com.

Baker Publishing Group publications use paper produced from sustainable forestry practices and postconsumer waste whenever possible.

25 26 27 28 29 30 31 7 6 5 4 3 2 1

To every girl who picks up this book—
I pray that your light shines brightly
in this world.

"Do everything without grumbling and arguing, so that you may be blameless and pure, children of God who are faultless in a crooked and perverted generation, among whom you shine like stars in the world."

Philippians 2:14–15

A note from Caroline Shankle

(also known as Melanie's daughter)

I write to you not as someone looking down on your situation, whatever that might be, but as the growing woman I am now *and* the girl I was. I write to you as someone who has been in the trenches, whether that meant mourning a lost friendship or being home with my parents on a Friday night because my group left me out. If you are currently messing up, feeling ashamed, or dealing with a heartbreak that hit you harder than you thought it would, I get it. I've experienced every bit of this. As I sit here and type this out, I am a twenty-one-year-old college student who is going into her spring semester with zero clue where her life will go. All I can do is trust God and be his humble servant.

I might not know your exact situation, but I know the fear, hurt, anger, and doubt you might be feeling. I have lived out those emotions before, and I'm living them out now. I want to write to you not from a distant pedestal of "do this" or "don't do that" but from the spot beside you in the trenches.

Whether it's lonely evenings, the days where you have a good cry in the bathroom stall at school, or the times you think that your head might explode if one more person tells you to "kill them with kindness"—we are all in the middle of a journey. We will face the lions and bears that God sends our way to prepare us for the giants we will face later on. We are the salt and the light of this world, but in order to make a difference, sometimes we have to face the hard conversations, the tough truths, and the battles that we just can't fight alone. But in these times, we are never alone. We have a God who loves us more than we can imagine and has plans for our lives that are beyond our wildest dreams.

A note from Melanie Shankle

(also known as Caroline's mom)

Caroline decided to write this devotional during one of the hardest seasons of her life. She was wrestling with God over what she had hoped and wanted life to look like and then she watched things work out much differently than the dreams she had in her head. Yet she had faith strong enough to know that God always opens a new door when he closes an old one, and the best thing she could do was walk faithfully through the open doors even when the way ahead looked scary and full of the unknown.

You may find yourself at a similar place in life and that's why you picked up this devotional as you try to find answers to some hard questions. Or maybe your mom picked it up for you because that's what moms do . . . we worry about our girls even as we fight to believe that God is going to work all things (even the hard things) for their good.

Regardless, here's a fact I can assure you of: God is writing a story for you that will probably look different at times than what you think you want, but it will always be the better story when you trust him and walk the path he has for you.

As Caroline wrote these entries, I read every word. Partly to help edit what she was writing but also because it gave me insight into her heart and all the ways God has been faithfully at work in her life. I hope you will find the same encouragement in her words that I found because what I saw over and over again was how God has continually given her the strength she has needed to fight all the lions and bears. It certainly hasn't been easy, but it has forged a resilience and grit in her that will serve her well for the rest of her life. And I promise you that whatever challenges you're facing, God will do the same in your life if you choose to trust him.

One of the things I admire most about Caroline is the way she sees people and situations for what they are deep down and how she isn't afraid to speak the truth to encourage the people around her to rise to the challenge of what God has called them to be. She has wisdom and discernment beyond her years, but she's also young enough to have recently gone through most of the struggles you may also find yourself facing right now. Through her words, I hope you'll see Caroline as a guide to help you navigate friendships, relationships, issues with self-image, knowing your worth, and how much Jesus loves you. But even more than that, I hope you'll see her as a friend who is praying for you and cheering you on down all the hard roads you may be walking because I can assure you, she will be. And I will be too.

Day 1

SMELLING LIKE SMOKE

DANIEL 3:27

And [they] . . . saw these men, upon whose bodies the fire had no power, nor was an hair of their head singed, neither were their coats changed, nor the smell of fire had passed on them. (KJV)

When I was a high school senior, I heard a sermon about Shadrach, Meshach, and Abednego where the pastor pointed out a detail in Daniel 3:27 I'd never noticed.

There was no smell of fire on them.

Everyone knows if you stand near a fire for even two minutes your hair will smell like smoke for days. If you've ever been to a Mexican restaurant, you know fajitas will make you smell of smoked meat basically for the rest of your life. But somehow these three biblical men trusted God enough to face the fire and came out not smelling like smoke. Guess what—you can too.

The pastor talked about how the smoke can represent bitterness and resentment. Anyone who has dealt with betrayal from people they thought were their friends knows there have been times, even after it was over, when they wished they could still clock [enter

person's name here] square in the nose. But instead of letting others win and have that much sway over us, let's think how we can walk through those trials and come out of them without harboring resentment or bitterness in our hearts.

Psalm 84:11–12 states: "For the Lord God is a sun and shield. The Lord grants favor and honor; he does not withhold the good from those who live with integrity. Happy is the person who trusts in you, Lord of Armies!"

We can remember that the Lord is working for our good. He delights in blessing us and delights in our joy. Wouldn't a God who is working all things in our favor also take care of the problems of our past? Sometimes all God wants to do is bless us, but if we are caught up in the bitterness of the past, we are unable to receive those blessings. I can recall times when I felt so hurt or wronged by a person and it just never seemed fair. The questions God brought to my heart were: "Even in this, do you believe I am still good? Do you trust me to be enough?"

The truth is that even when the people we care about hurt us or let us down, God is sufficient. He is our daily bread, and he will always take care of us when others fall short. Why should we harbor anger or grief when God has something so much greater planned for us? We can go through a trial smelling like smoke or we can come out unscathed. We can pick up our cross, learn what we can from the hardship, and step into the inheritance God has for us.

Why should we harbor anger or grief when God has something so much greater planned for us?

Day 2

A DIFFERENT SEASON, A DIFFERENT DESIGN

ISAIAH 43:19

Look, I am about to do something new;
even now it is coming. Do you not see it?

Throughout life, friendships will ebb and flow. When we are young, we see movies or hear stories of friend groups that last forever, and we naturally believe that is a normal thing. The reality is having friends that last forever is so rare. I thought it was normal until I reached high school and saw the natural high school food chain cause a million friend groups to implode, including mine. I say implode but honestly there are a myriad of ways a friend group can fall apart, and I've definitely experienced a few of them.

You might be in a group that decides to cut you out (ouch). Maybe one girl starts spreading rumors about you (not fun), or maybe y'all just start to grow up and become very different, which creates distance. No matter what happens though, it hurts. You feel lonely or abandoned. You may even wonder what's wrong with you when this is

happening. As someone who has been through it and will most likely go through it again, I want to tell you that sometimes it's not about you—or even them. Often, it's more about what God has planned for you and how he wants you to grow.

The people we spend our time with influence us heavily, even if we don't realize it. For example, I live with one of my best friends, Lyndi, and the way we have picked up each other's mannerisms and dialect should be studied. Sometimes we don't say anything, but with just a random noise or look, we immediately know what the other one is thinking. This can be a good thing, but sometimes imitating those close to you can hold you back or prevent growth. When that happens, something has to change.

It hurts to lose people you care about or to have to walk away from friendships, but sometimes it's the right thing. God desires each of us to reach our full potential in him. He puts us in different seasons for a reason. Some seasons, we need to have people in our lives who are pushing us to grow. In other seasons, we need people who are comforting and encouraging. But no matter which season we are in, we need people in our lives who are going to walk with us in a way that is uplifting and honoring to the Lord.

God desires each of us to reach our full potential in him. He puts us in different seasons for a reason.

Day 3

WHEN TO WALK AWAY

PROVERBS 27:17

As iron sharpens iron,
so one person sharpens another. (NIV)

If the people around you are more like rubber than iron, then, as the verse tells us, they will not help sharpen you. You cannot grow from their influence. I have struggled with this in my life. Sometimes letting go hurts a lot, especially when you really, really want to make something work. This can happen with a friendship or even in a relationship. I have brought my hurt to God, and I know he wants all things good for me. But in the same way a toddler doesn't know any better and would eat candy until they're sick, I have wanted things that God has refused to give me because he is always working for my good.

There was one time when I brought my hurt to God and asked, "Why? Why won't you let this work? Why am I so exhausted trying to do what I think is the right thing?" The response God gave me was so clear. All I felt was a statement in my heart: "You cannot carry someone through the door you are supposed to walk through." As

much as we want to be the iron that God uses to sharpen another person, we are sometimes called to walk away from relationships because they are dragging us down instead of lifting us up.

Most of the time, waiting for those open doors is a battle. Yes, God will equip you. And yes, God will give you strength. He will give you all that you need for *you* to walk through that open door. Many times, God has made it apparent to me that I am not called to try to carry someone with me. I understand the pain of changing friend groups and walking away from people you care about. I have shed lots of tears over these very things. But what would be even more painful than God removing unequally yoked people from my life would be trying to diminish my purpose and to stay with those around me if he's calling me to move on.

If God is taking something away from you or if you have to walk away from friendships, just know that it is because there is something so much better in store for you on the other side. God loves you and his desire is to bless you. So focus on him; be hopeful and excited for the new season and the people he will bring into your life when the time is right.

God will give you all that you need for you to walk through that open door.

Day 4

THE LION AND THE BEAR

HEBREWS 12:11

No discipline seems pleasant at the time, but painful. Later on, however, it produces a harvest of righteousness and peace for those who have been trained by it. (NIV)

I don't think we fully understand or appreciate what life was like for a shepherd many centuries ago. We read about them, and it seems like they lead pretty simple lives. Take care of sheep, protect the flock, make sure there's something to eat, and then maybe get visited in the middle of the night by a choir of angels declaring the Savior's birth. Fairly easy, right?

Let me tell you, as an animal science major who has had to deal with sheep, I have a whole new appreciation for shepherds. It's almost comical to me now that God compares us to sheep because, my goodness, sheep are dumb. And I don't mean dumb like your sweet golden retriever. I mean dumb like they will dive face-first into a ditch you literally just pulled them out of and get stuck again. And then you pull them out again and guess what? They get stuck a third time. It's ridiculous.

When thinking about shepherds, David immediately comes to mind. He was the youngest of eight sons, thrown out in the wilderness alone to take care of these sheep that I now know run toward the face of danger. Can you imagine being in the dark all by yourself with a flock and then being the only thing between them and a hungry predator? Kind of terrifying, in my opinion. We know for a fact that David had to face down a lion and a bear.

We will all face our version of a lion and a bear in life. For me, there have been times when I have been so put out or discouraged. Moments when I got injured again or girls said hurtful things to me and I had to have tough conversations. Any time I would vent or talk about it with my parents, my dad would always say the same words: "The lion and the bear." When he said that, I would kind of get it. I knew that things would be okay later on and it would all work out, just like it did for David. But it took me a while to realize that so many of the things I went through were not just trials but preparation for what was ahead. God was preparing me for so many things that I will face later on in life. He was giving me the grit and resilience I would need. He was teaching me to trust in his ability to give me the strength and wisdom to fight future battles. Just as God gave David the lion and the bear before he had to face down Goliath, God gives each of us our own refining trials.

Just as God gave David the lion and the bear before he had to face down Goliath, God gives each of us our own refining trials.

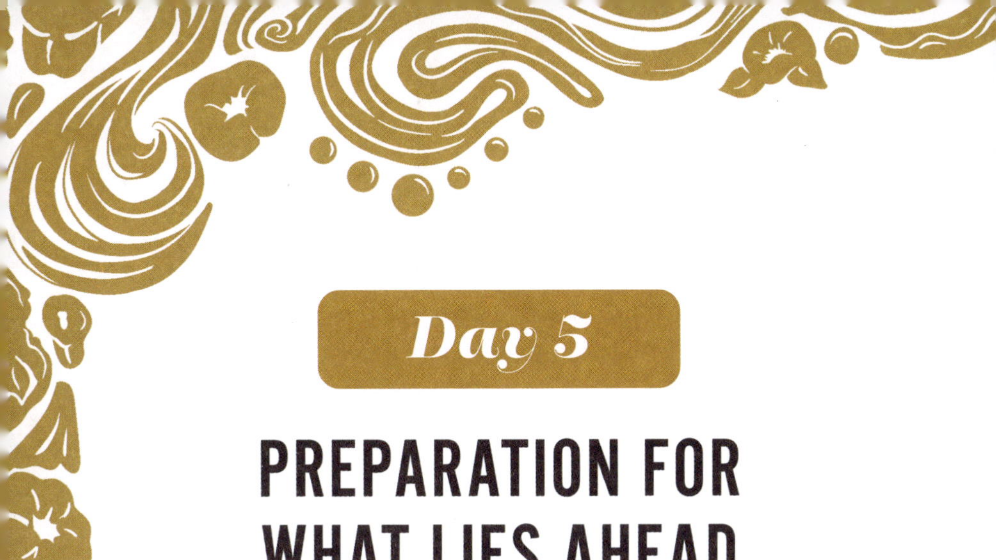

Day 5

PREPARATION FOR WHAT LIES AHEAD

1 SAMUEL 17:34–37

David said, "I've been a shepherd, tending sheep for my father. Whenever a lion or bear came and took a lamb from the flock, I'd go after it, knock it down, and rescue the lamb. . . . And I'll do the same to this Philistine pig who is taunting the troops of God-Alive. God, who delivered me from the teeth of the lion and the claws of the bear, will deliver me from this Philistine." (MSG)

While fighting off the lion and the bear to protect his sheep, David had to rely on a strength greater than his own. He had to put faith in God to help him protect the lambs. Now, does that mean he was as cool as a cucumber and ready to go when he had to face Goliath? Probably not. He still had to place his faith over his fear. But here's the thing: He already knew how to do that because God had given him battles where he had to practice. David had proven to be faithful; he was ready to defend his people and his nation.

The blueprint of David's story repeated throughout his life. God had a purpose for every challenge David faced. In his early days

of being a shepherd, David knew that to protect his flock he had to keep placing his faith in the Lord. But when Goliath showed up, David likely realized the reason for all the previous battles he had fought. God knew David would face Goliath one day and that he would need to know exactly how big God was and know that he had been equipped for this moment. The only thing that changed was the stakes became higher.

The same thing can be said for us. God gives us our own lions and bears to face. I had to overcome many struggles in high school to learn how to place my faith in something greater than myself. I had to learn and practice how to gain strength from God and God alone. As I get further out of high school, I look back at those times that were lonely or that just straight-up sucked. Were they fun? No, definitely not. But have they prepared me for so many struggles that I've encountered? Absolutely.

God is always working to prepare us for a future that we cannot see, and he is building strength in us to face whatever will come our way, knowing that he is always on our side.

God is always working to prepare us for a future that we cannot see.

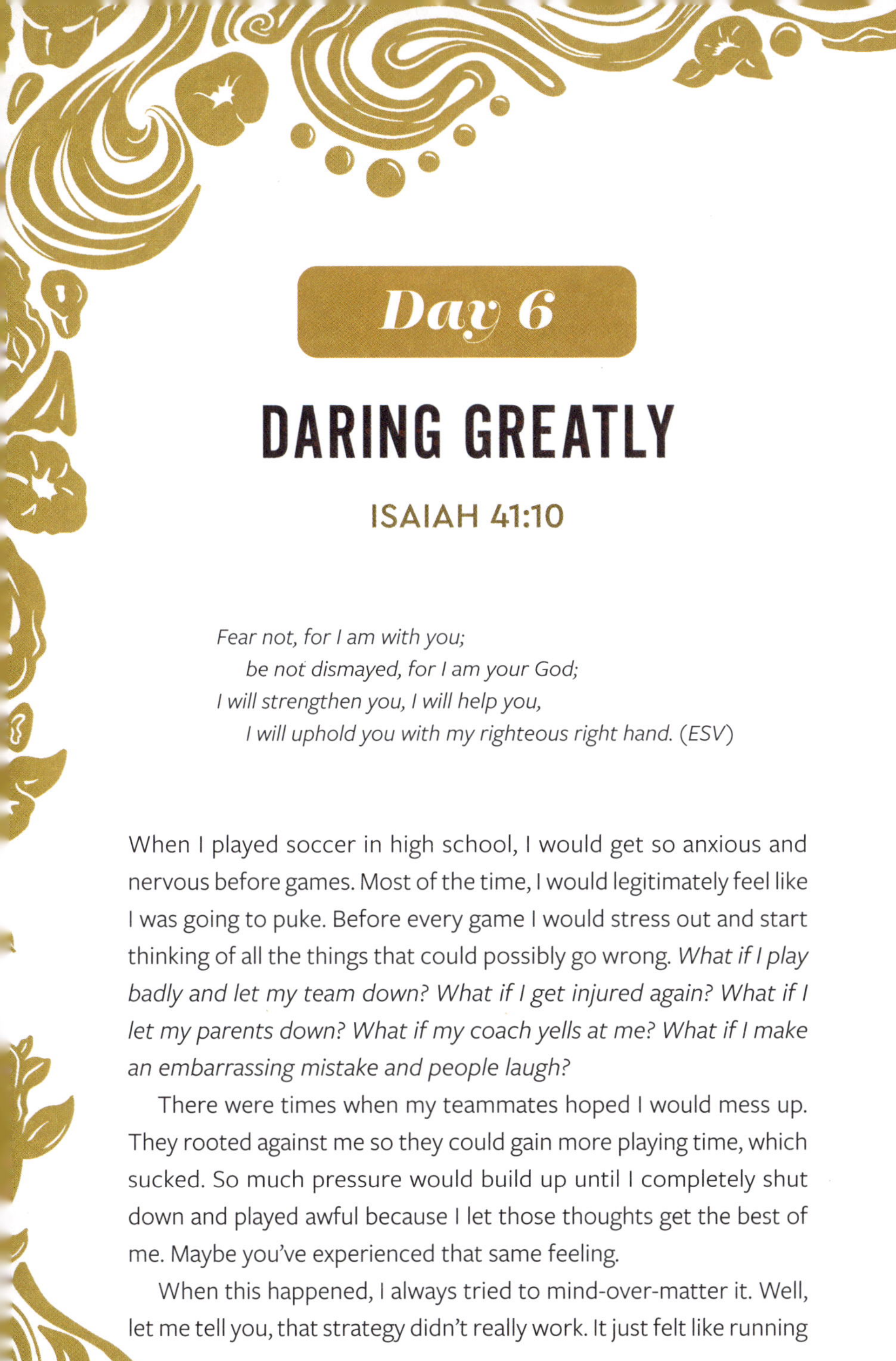

Day 6

DARING GREATLY

ISAIAH 41:10

Fear not, for I am with you;
be not dismayed, for I am your God;
I will strengthen you, I will help you,
I will uphold you with my righteous right hand. (ESV)

When I played soccer in high school, I would get so anxious and nervous before games. Most of the time, I would legitimately feel like I was going to puke. Before every game I would stress out and start thinking of all the things that could possibly go wrong. *What if I play badly and let my team down? What if I get injured again? What if I let my parents down? What if my coach yells at me? What if I make an embarrassing mistake and people laugh?*

There were times when my teammates hoped I would mess up. They rooted against me so they could gain more playing time, which sucked. So much pressure would build up until I completely shut down and played awful because I let those thoughts get the best of me. Maybe you've experienced that same feeling.

When this happened, I always tried to mind-over-matter it. Well, let me tell you, that strategy didn't really work. It just felt like running into a brick wall over and over again. But you know what silenced those doubts and anxieties? The truth. Telling myself the truth over and over again.

There is a specific quote that I have carried with me since high school, and it's from a speech by Theodore Roosevelt.

> It is not the critic who counts; not the man who points out how the strong man stumbles. . . . The credit belongs to the man who is actually in the arena, whose face is marred by dust and sweat and blood; who strives valiantly; who errs, who comes short again and again.*

While this is not inherently biblical, it is what our whole faith is based on. We are not remotely called to perfection. We are called to fight valiantly for our faith. For us, it's not about our worldly success or the opinions of others but how hard we strive in our race for Christ.

Our identity isn't in our failure; it's in how many times we get up after the failure. No matter where you are, whether it's competing for a sport, studying for school, or standing up for yourself and what you believe in, God will uphold you. He will give you strength. That is the truth I hold on to when doubts creep in. So do not be afraid of the opinions of others or dismayed at the thought of failing. Your identity and worth are in God and God alone. That truth is where we find the courage to dare and dare greatly.

Your identity and worth are in God and God alone.

---

* Theodore Roosevelt, *Citizenship in a Republic*. Speech, Sorbonne, Paris, April 23, 1910, https://www.theodorerooseveltcenter.org/Learn-About-TR/TR-Encyclopedia/Culture-and-Society/Man-in-the-Arena.aspx.

Day 7

THE WEEKLY RECAP

Five Truths to Remember:

1. We should not harbor anger or grief when God has something so much greater planned for us.
2. God delights in blessing us and wants us to have joy.
3. God desires for each of us to reach our full potential. He puts us through different seasons for a reason.
4. If God is taking something away from us or asking us to walk away from friendships, know that he has something so much better in store on the other side.
5. Just as God gave David the lion and the bear before he had to face down Goliath, God gives us obstacles of our own to overcome—with his power.

Three Questions to Ask:

1. Are you holding on to any anger or grief right now? With God's help, how can you start letting it go?

2. Can you think of a situation or a relationship that God may be asking you to walk away from because it is hurting you?

3. What are some of the lions and bears you have faced in your life? How did you handle them?

Day 8

GOD KNOWS WHAT HE HAS FOR US

JEREMIAH 29:11

"For I know the plans I have for you," declares the Lord, "plans to prosper you and not to harm you, plans to give you hope and a future." (NIV)

Starting college was a learning curve for me. It was legitimately so exciting, and I had a blast, but there were a few adjustments I wasn't expecting. It was very weird to get there and realize that almost everyone around me was just as accomplished as me, if not more so. We all made good grades in high school, had good records, and were very involved and highly motivated. While this was a good thing, it led to a lot of comparison issues for me.

Most people in my major had more experience than me. They grew up in the livestock world and knew so much more about it. There were days when I felt so behind. I tried my best to blend in and get the experience I needed, but I still compared myself to everyone else, and I always came up short. But God blessed me with

some amazing friends who helped me learn their world and a couple professors who truly cared about their students.

One day I was talking with a professor, and I admitted, "I don't know what I'm going to do in this industry." I explained how I was really stressed because I didn't have the internships, experience, or opportunities that some of my friends did.

He looked at me and said, "Comparison is the thief of joy." I thought this was so wise and poetic, and I admired that he had the wit to put such a profound concept in such a succinct way. I later found out he was quoting Theodore Roosevelt, but I still like to credit my professor in my heart.

One of the biggest traps we fall into is the terrible habit of comparing everyone's best parts to our worst parts. So, of course, we always come up short and feel bad about ourselves. We are all completely different people with completely different callings. Often the reason female friendships end is because someone falls prey to the trap of comparison. As girls it is so easy to let that side of ourselves win. In reality, God has plans for all of us to prosper. He wants to give us hope and a future, and it's not going to be the same hope and future as he gives the people around us. Thank God for that. How boring it would be if we all had the same story!

God has an amazing purpose for the unique person he created you to be. Someone else's blessing does not mean a lack of your own.

God has an amazing purpose for the unique person he created you to be.

Day 9

LETTING GO OF COMPARISON

GALATIANS 5:26

We will not compare ourselves with each other as if one of us were better and another worse. We have far more interesting things to do with our lives. Each of us is an original. (MSG)

Currently, all my friends and I are gearing up to go into the "real world," as the "real adults" like to say. It has been such a crazy experience to watch everyone around me grow up. I look back to who we were freshman year and who we are now, and all of us have changed so much. Moreover, even all my friends in my major are doing completely different things.

As I've looked back on the earlier years of college, I've started to wonder what I would go back and tell myself, and here is what I came up with: No one actually knows what's going on. People love to act like they have it all together, and some girl named Bethany is definitely going to brag about triple majoring while on a presidential scholarship, but don't let that make you feel less than. Remember, comparison is the thief of joy. You are just fine where you are, and I promise you everyone is just acting like they have it together.

You're not alone and you're not behind. You're right where you need to be. My friends and I walked into college so naive about God's plans for us. We would get jealous, be overly competitive, and put ourselves in boxes trying to fit this perfect mold. Then we started to realize we each have different strengths, which will lead us on different paths. The times I have been the worst at something are when I've let comparison get the best of me and tried to excel at someone else's strength.

Now, I have friends in Washington, DC, who are working in congressional houses. Some are helping with surgeries on animals in South Africa, others have internships all over the nation, and I'm here writing this devotional. We are all in the same major and yet we're all playing to our own strengths. Each of us is making an impact on the world in our unique way.

The only reason that is possible is because we stopped trying to be like everyone else around us. We chose the life the Spirit has for us and have been blessed with contentment and fruit only found by abiding in Christ. Each of us is an original, meant for our own path, but we'll never be able to fully reach our potential or discover our own strengths if we are all caught up in comparing ourselves to others.

You're not alone and you're not behind. You're right where you need to be.

Day 10

THE POWER OF VULNERABILITY

1 JOHN 1:7

But if we walk in the light, God himself being the light, we also experience a shared life with one another, as the sacrificed blood of Jesus, God's Son, purges all our sin. (MSG)

In high school it can feel like we're the only one in the world who is hurting or struggling. And that is exactly how the enemy wants us to feel. That we are alone in our sorrow, our sin, our shame, our hurt. Satan wants us to feel isolated because when we think we are alone, our spirit is low. It is his greatest weapon against us. It's why we feel scared to be vulnerable or honest about our struggles.

When our hurt is hidden in the shadows, we stay weak because there is no one who can speak truth and light over that pain. When I was struggling, I always believed I had to stay strong to keep up the image that I was totally fine. I didn't think it was normal to struggle, and I thought that I should be able to get over it and move on. Because maybe my struggles and failures were a sign that I wasn't a

strong enough Christian. Then, the August before my freshman year of college, I went to a camp called Impact, which is a Christian camp meant to plug incoming students at my university into the body of Christ. For the first time in my life, I saw people my own age taking their faith seriously. I saw my generation rallying around and encouraging each other. It was incredible. One day every girl counselor in my cabin shared their testimonies, and you want to know what? Every single one of them was broken.

This is the power of truth and vulnerability. It is a scary thing, but it has the power to move mountains. If those girls at camp hadn't had the courage to share their testimonies and be vulnerable, then I might still be trapped in my doubts and insecurities. Their vulnerability led to my freedom. So what I will leave you with on this day is that sometimes bringing something out of the darkness and into the light can be terrifying, but there is freedom in living in the truth and in embracing our imperfection. All of us are broken and imperfect, but the difference is whether we are willing to take the leap of faith to bring what lies in the shadows into the light. Do not underestimate the power of sharing your story and how your honesty can change the lives of others.

Do not underestimate the power of sharing your story and how your honesty can change the lives of others.

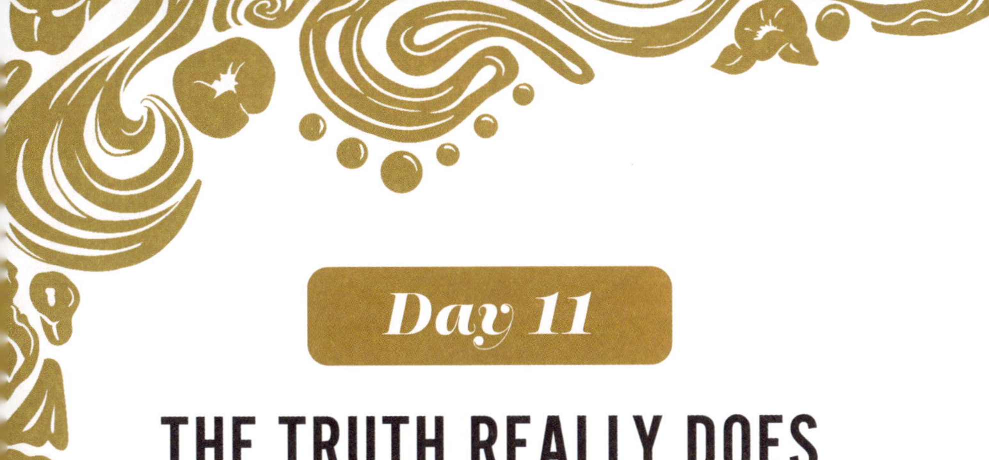

Day 11

THE TRUTH REALLY DOES SET YOU FREE

1 THESSALONIANS 5:11

Therefore encourage one another and build each other up, just as in fact you are doing. (NIV)

The incredible Christian women I met during Impact had different struggles, doubts, insecurities, sins, and failures. But one thing they all had in common was that God met them exactly where they were. He didn't meet them after they got it together or once they made themselves look better. He met them at their lowest.

These girls were so honest and vulnerable that they brought all the sin that trapped them into the light, and they let God set them free. Their identity wasn't in their failures but in Christ. Knowing this took a massive weight off my shoulders. For the first time in my life, I wasn't alone in how I felt. All these women had once felt exactly the same way I did. And they had embraced God's love instead of trying to work for it. They'd been courageous enough to step into the light. During those few days of camp, I was finally able to be vulnerable and honest. Once my struggles were voiced and in the open, they didn't seem as daunting as they had in the silence. Moreover, I now had a group of women who could lift me up in prayer, and we could rally for each other in our struggles. Never underestimate how powerful it is to have people in your life who will pray for and encourage you.

It is said in John 8:32 that "the truth will set you free," and that is the reality of any situation. The moment you speak the lies the enemy has told you out loud and cover them in the light of truth, you are free. You do not have to earn God's love or work toward it. You are not helpless; you are not hopeless. You are loved, you are chosen, you are set apart in your weakness, you are strong, and you are a daughter of the King Most High.

This is the power of truth and vulnerability. It is scary, but it can move mountains. Bringing something from the darkness into the light can be terrifying, but there is freedom in living in the truth, however imperfect. Do not underestimate the power of your story and how your honesty will change the lives of others.

Bringing something from the darkness into the light can be terrifying, but there is freedom in living in the truth, however imperfect.

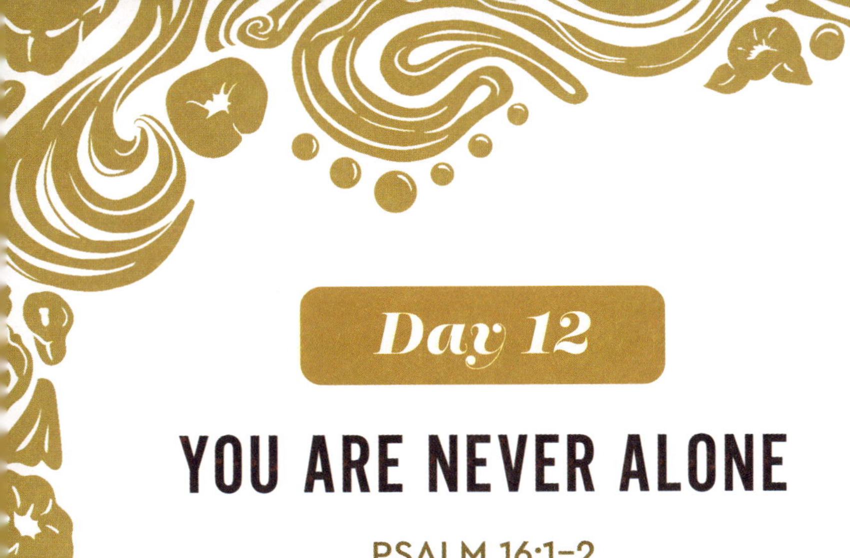

Day 12

YOU ARE NEVER ALONE

PSALM 16:1–2

Protect me, God, for I take refuge in you.
I said to the Lord, "You are my Lord;
I have nothing good besides you."

No matter how many women I talk to, I've found that all have had an experience dealing with mean girls and losing friendships. They're such normal things to go through, yet for some reason no one talks about it.

In college I talk with my friends about their mean girl experiences. We all reluctantly agree that yes, girls can be pretty mean. But no one discusses how isolating and lonely that can feel. And while I was in the middle of high school drama, I would've rather died than admit mean girls were getting to me. It sucked though, and I felt really lonely at some points. All I wanted was one person who was loyal to me and understood me. I hated not having that.

I know it sounds like a cliché that God is always with you and you are never alone, but this is true. You are never alone, and God always has your back, no matter what. I know—when you're eating lunch

alone or crying at home on a Friday night because everyone went out without you, it still feels like you're on your own.

But look ahead. God sees the bigger picture, and we can choose to view our painful situations from his perspective. I was eventually able to bond over those hard times with some of my college friends. During those times, God was forging a strength and resilience in me. I am so much more independent and confident because I had to trust God to be with me during the lonely times. I took refuge in him. It hurt and I still felt crappy, but I could talk to God about those feelings. I could pray for a future when I would find some good friends. This season also helped me grow in my relationship with Christ.

I hear so many Christians talk about being lonely and how spending time with God is the "sweetest, most awesome thing." I will say that spending time with God in hardships is so incredible and you can feel his love, but loneliness still hurts. Spending time with God in our loneliness is more like working out. In the middle of the workout, you want to puke and probably hate it, but the accomplishment when you finish and the endurance you gain is great in the long run.

If on your loneliest days you make God your source, real fruit will be produced. As it says in Psalm 16:2, "I have nothing good besides you." All goodness comes from him. So while you might not be able to see it in these current hard moments, look ahead. You are laying the foundation for your future.

If on your loneliest days you make God your source, real fruit will be produced.

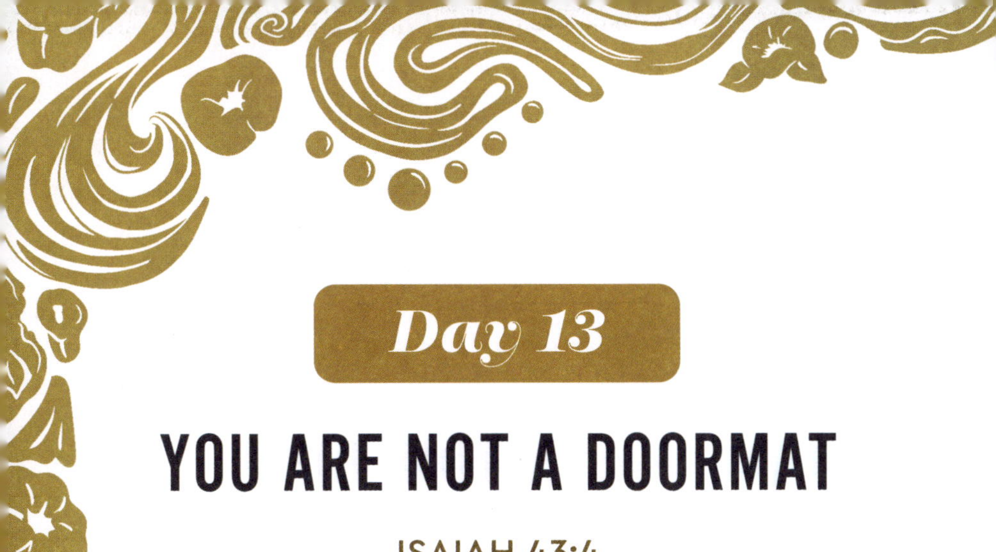

Day 13

YOU ARE NOT A DOORMAT

ISAIAH 43:4

You are precious in my eyes,
and honored, and I love you. (ESV)

One of the biggest traps we fall into when dealing with conflict is thinking we need to "keep the peace." It seems like everyone I know feels this deep obligation to try to make everybody happy. They don't want to rock the boat. They are intimidated by the fallout or the idea of someone not liking them.

There absolutely is a time to take the high road and avoid the drama. I tried so hard to do that in my sophomore year of high school, and it just didn't work. There were some girls in my life and in my old friend group who were being toxic. They were rude and tore me down instead of building me up. I blocked these girls on social media and cut off ties with anyone connected with them, but they would follow me into a bathroom or try to instigate more conflict. Adults told me to kill them with kindness and just try to ignore them. Unfortunately, it only got worse and all I wanted to do was wait until one of them cornered me, then maybe start a boxing match. But that's not quite what Jesus would do. I felt so unlike myself and like I wasn't being true to who I was.

One night I came home upset and told my parents that trying to keep the peace wasn't working and trying to be nice didn't help at all. My dad, with one of his typical calm reactions, looked at me and said, "This means war."

At that moment, a light bulb went off for me. I am precious and honored in God's eyes. I have value and worth and self-respect. And "keeping the peace" in this situation was not honoring God at all.

These girls were speaking horrible things over me and, even worse, I was believing what they said. Psalm 18:39–40 says, "You have clothed me with strength for battle; you subdue my adversaries beneath me. You have made my enemies retreat before me." Does that sound like God wants us to be a doormat for the sake of not making a few people angry?

There is a way to stand up and advocate for ourselves in all of the drama without becoming the drama. I learned to take my feelings out of the equation. I allowed myself to be grounded in logic and speak the truth. I was able to confront those girls in a way that kept me above reproach. Soon after I stood my ground, they left me alone. Even better, I had a new sense of self-respect that came from knowing my worth in Christ and the way he made me.

We are precious and honored in God's eyes. We have value and worth and self-respect.

THE WEEKLY RECAP

Five Truths to Remember:

1. God has an amazing purpose that is totally unique to each of us and our gifts.
2. We will never reach our potential or discover our own path if we spend all our time comparing ourselves to someone else.
3. There is power and truth in being honest and vulnerable with others.
4. We are never alone. God is always with us.
5. We can advocate for ourselves amid drama without becoming the drama.

Three Questions to Ask:

1. What gifts or talents do you feel God has given you?

2. How can you work toward focusing on who God created you to be and not comparing yourself to those around you?

3. Where can you stand up and advocate for yourself or someone else and be a peacemaker?

Day 15

FACING REJECTION

ROMANS 8:28

We know that all things work together for the good of those who love God, who are called according to his purpose.

In life, we have to get used to rejection. It is such a normal part of life, but for some reason in our heads and in our culture, we villainize it. There have been so many times I have been guilty of making rejection and failure synonyms, when, in reality, they are not quite the same. This was most visible to me when I was applying to organizations or clubs in college. There was one student organization in particular that I really wanted to be a part of, but I didn't get in. Honestly, I wasn't used to rejection like that, and it threw me off. I kept overthinking every aspect of that rejection and naturally concluded that I was an absolute failure to my bloodline and that nobody wanted me in the organization because I wasn't good enough. I mean, that was the obvious answer.

Okay. No. That was most definitely not the answer.

That's what my insecurities wanted me to think.

Now I had two different paths I could take. Option one was to throw a pity party and never put myself back out there because what

if I failed and got rejected again? This is what I call a victim mentality. We are all guilty of it sometimes. Option two was to change my perspective, quiet down the doubts in my mind, and put myself back out there to see what God had for me. What I mean when I say "change my perspective" is that I needed to come to the realization that getting rejected is not the equivalent of failing.

God is working all things together for his glory and our good. This includes the times things don't go our way. Because I got rejected from that student organization, I applied to a different one, and I met some of my best friends and had some incredible experiences I never would have had otherwise. Moreover, God was able to work through me in a way that was so much better than what I had planned for myself.

Rejection is not failure; it is redirection. Take rejection as encouragement that you are one step closer to the right thing. Doors are going to close on you and that's okay because that means another one will open. Don't be so focused on the closed door that you miss the others that God opened right next to it.

Rejection is not failure;
it is redirection.

Day 16

FINDING PURPOSE IN FAILURE

2 CORINTHIANS 12:9

But he said to me, "My grace is sufficient for you, for my power is made perfect in weakness." Therefore I will boast all the more gladly about my weaknesses, so that Christ's power may rest on me." (NIV)

Yesterday we talked about not villainizing rejection and how it means redirection, not failure. Today let's talk about failure. Just like rejection, failure is also a normal thing, yet most of us are scared of it. We look at it as something inherently bad—something that automatically makes all our doubts and insecurities come true. Usually that leads us to avoid things because we *might* fail.

Don't avoid something for the fear of failing or not doing it perfectly. Failure is inevitable; it will happen. My freshman year of college my chemistry professor purposely set us up for failure. Most of us were A-plus students in high school who didn't really have to study to get good grades. We thought college would be the same. My first grade in chemistry was a 13 out of 100. That's as bad as you think it

is. My professor knew we would all totally bomb the test, but it gave us a much-needed reality check. I learned how to study real quick and never got a 13 on a test again. Did it suck to fail that first exam? Yeah, it was not fun. But it prepared me for the rest of that course and taught me how necessary studying was in college. If my professor had nicely asked us to study, I never would have, and it would have been a rude awakening when it actually mattered.

I feel that's how God uses all the failures in our lives. In our weakness, his power is perfected. His grace is demonstrated when we fall short, and then we learn.

God knows we are inherently stubborn beings. Just as my chemistry professor knew his students had to figure out for ourselves why it was important to study, God knows that we have to learn a lot of different facets of life. Luckily, our God is full of grace and mercy. He is going to let us stumble and fail sometimes, but he will always be there to pick us back up. And usually whatever we learn from those failures is going to be crucial later on in our stories.

Do not fear inevitable failure; don't let fear stop you from getting out and doing that hard thing or taking that risk. Think about all the lessons you're missing out on when you play it safe. Think about all the ways you will be able to improve. Remember that God is walking in that failure right beside you, ready to pick you back up and help you do it better next time. It's often our failures that God uses to set us up for greater successes down the line.

It's often our failures that God uses to set us up for greater successes down the line.

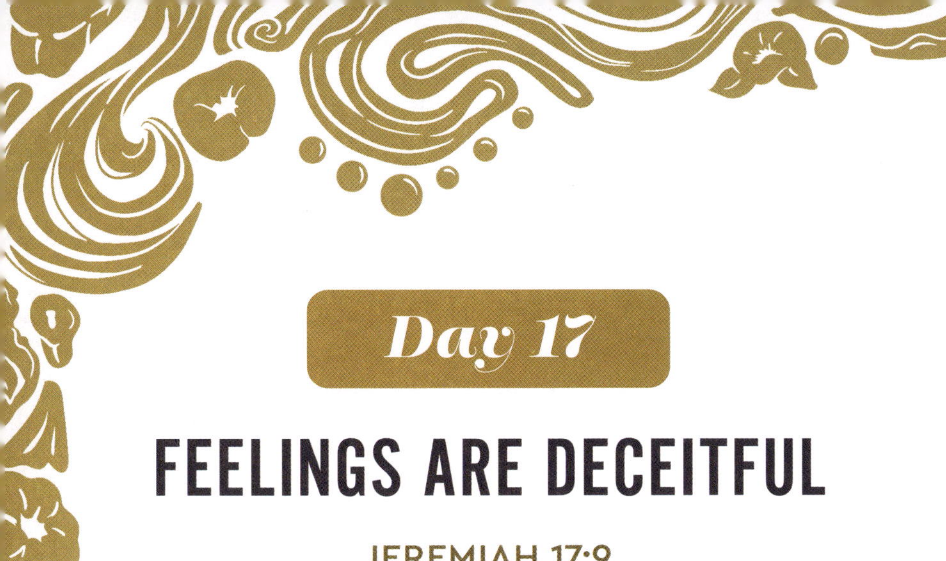

Day 17

FEELINGS ARE DECEITFUL

JEREMIAH 17:9

The heart is more deceitful than anything else,
and incurable—who can understand it?

Feelings are such a difficult thing to handle. They are so complex and change on the turn of a dime. We never really have a handle on them, and they constantly mislead us, yet they influence us so easily. We live in a day and age when, according to the world, our feelings should rule us. The priority is always "How does that make you feel?" or "How are you feeling?" Meanwhile, the Bible clearly states that our feelings are of the flesh and that our hearts deceive us. It is so frustrating.

On the other side of the spectrum, I have seen Christians blatantly lie about their feelings. They ignore the reality of their situation completely and bottle up every emotion, saying that everything is amazing because God is amazing—duh—when in reality they're holding on by a thread.

I can't help but think there has to be a balance. I mean, the book of Lamentations does exist. Even though our hearts can be deceitful,

we are still allowed to acknowledge what it is they are saying. We can't give our feelings power to rule over our actions. The thing that helps us overpower a lie is to bring it into the light, so shouldn't we do that with our feelings as well?

I look back at some of the hard times I have gone through. They never felt amazing and there were lots of tears shed, but I still knew that God was working in those moments. I always knew deep down that, in the end, this was what would be best for me, even if my heart didn't understand it.

When I had lonely nights or experienced hard times, I learned that I needed to acknowledge what I felt. There were so many times I wished I could just ignore my feelings, but whenever I tried it usually ended in everything coming out all at once. The key is not to let your feelings rule your life. Do not make your decision based on how you feel because our hearts are deceitful. Look toward the Bible and not your heart for ways to walk in truth and wisdom in your life and the decisions you make.

Look toward the Bible and not your heart for ways to walk in truth and wisdom in your life and the decisions you make.

Day 18

PERFECTIONISM

ROMANS 3:23–24

For all have sinned and fall short of the glory of God; they are justified freely by his grace through the redemption that is in Christ Jesus.

I hate screwing something up, and I hate it even more when I can't fix something myself. Funnily enough, that's kind of the whole basis of Christianity. We serve a perfect God and yet we constantly mess things up that we can't fix alone. For so long I thought I was just bad at being a Christian. The reality is we will all mess up. Something I tell myself after messing up is, "The good news is the Lord has factored in my stupidity with his plan." God doesn't expect us to get things right on the first try. That's the whole reason Christ died for us—to walk in our place as the perfect human so all we have to do is live by faith and keep our eyes on him, even after we screw things up.

I played soccer from first grade through high school. I loved everything about the game—the intensity, the teamwork, and the way it forced me to push myself to be better. But I went through a season where I became so afraid of making a mistake that I quit playing the way I'd always played. Instead of instinctively taking a header

or diving to kick the ball in the goal, I mentally calculated the odds of doing something wrong. I was trying to play an imperfect game with perfection, and it caused me to compromise the very skills that made me a good player.

One night during dinner, my parents talked with me about my most recent game and said it just didn't seem like I was playing the way I usually did. I confessed that I was afraid of messing up and it was affecting me. My dad said something that changed everything: "No one is asking you to be perfect. We are asking you to play to the best of your ability. Failure is inevitable so go out on that field, give it everything you have, and don't be afraid to fail spectacularly. I'd rather see you try and fail than not try at all."

I believe that's how God views us. He knows we aren't going to get it right every time, but he cares more about our heart than our performance. He wants us to listen to his voice and follow where he leads, but he knows there are times that we are going to get it wrong.

So rest in that truth and do not focus on being perfect. Instead, focus on being faithful to follow where he leads. God calls us to abide faithfully, not perfectly.

God wants us to listen to his voice and follow where he leads, but he knows there are times that we are going to get it wrong.

Day 19

WHY YOU ARE THE WAY YOU ARE

PSALM 139:16

Your eyes saw me when I was formless;
all my days were written in your book and planned
before a single one of them began.

I would love to be a lighthearted, free-spirit kind of girl who just rolls with things, but that is not how God wired my personality. I like to be in charge of things so I can prepare for every outcome and hopefully not get hurt in the process. For me, that tendency is rooted in self-preservation or protection. This is probably one of the biggest lies I often let myself believe, because the reality is I have so little control over so many things. Maybe this is something you struggle with even if you don't realize it.

There was a time in my life when I would talk with a person or finish a social interaction, then go home and replay that scenario over and over and overthink every little thing. Sometimes I would try to dress in a way so that people wouldn't judge me, and I would keep

up with the trends just to stay in touch—and sometimes I would do this funny thing where I would try to act so chill and nonchalant to people because I thought if I came off as too eager, they wouldn't like me as much.

Even now, at twenty-one, I'm guilty of trying to control people's perception of me sometimes. I worry that I come off as too much because I really do care about the things around me. I'm not a chill person, I can be loud and maybe a smidgeon overemotional at times, and I get scared that people will see that and not want anything to do with me. So I think, *Maybe if I control how much of my true self people see, they will stay around.* But I hold no control over other people's opinions of me. At some point if they don't appreciate the real version of me, they'll still leave and all I'll have done is lie to myself and them.

Remember, God made you exactly as you are supposed to be, right now. One person may not like something about you, but there's another person who will absolutely adore that part of your personality. Your relationships will fall into place exactly how God wills them to. There is nothing you can do to keep around a person who has no place in your life. So what I'm still learning and what I would encourage you with is to be your full self. The people who are meant to stick around absolutely will, no matter what, and they will love you fully just as God created you. Don't let the illusion of control stop you from being completely authentic to those around you. Embrace all that God created you to be.

Don't let the illusion of control stop you from being completely authentic to those around you.

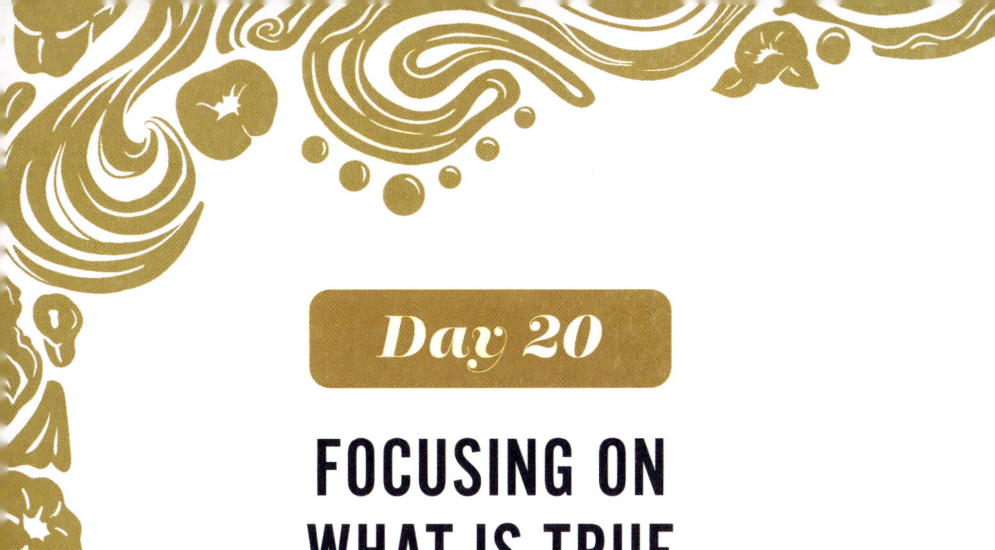

Day 20

FOCUSING ON WHAT IS TRUE

PHILIPPIANS 4:8–9

You'll do best by filling your minds and meditating on things true, noble, reputable, authentic, compelling, gracious—the best, not the worst; the beautiful, not the ugly; things to praise, not things to curse. (MSG)

A few months ago, I went through a really hard heartbreak. I was let down, hurt, and betrayed. I had so much anger toward people and toward God. In my head, I had just lost the guy I thought I was going to spend the rest of my life with. There was one moment that was particularly rough. It felt like I had so many things stacked up against me, and it all felt so unfair. I didn't understand why God let me date someone who would make me feel like that. I was mad that God didn't just snap his fingers and fix this whole mess. I was also mad at myself for caring so much for someone who would end up completely letting me down. I focused on all the sadness and anger, and at some point I realized staying on this path was only causing me to spiral.

Nothing good can come from the would'ves, could'ves, and should'ves in life. The last time I had felt so bad was my sophomore year of high school. During that year, I remember praying so hard to make it to college and to have real, true friendships with loyal and loving people.

Fast-forward to a-few-months-ago me, heartbroken and crying on the bathroom floor. I realized that even though the heartbreak hurt so bad, I was overlooking all the prayers God had answered in my life. I was so focused on one boy who broke my heart that I wasn't paying attention to the incredible friends helping me through this heartbreak. I really had been looking at all that God hadn't done for me yet (key word *yet*) and not focusing on all that God had already done for me in his faithfulness.

Once I started to focus on God's goodness throughout my life and not just on my current struggle, things started to change. I was able to be joyful, have hope, and heal. It gave me perspective to appreciate all that I have and not just get frustrated at what I didn't have or what didn't work out.

So, in times when things are difficult and the negatives start creeping in, remember the good and think about God's faithfulness in other areas or aspects of your life. If God hasn't given you one desire yet, look toward the different ones that he has fulfilled and know that if he can be faithful there, he will be faithful everywhere else too.

If God hasn't given you one desire yet, look toward the different ones that he has fulfilled and know that if he can be faithful there, he will be faithful everywhere else too.

Day 21

THE WEEKLY RECAP

Five Truths to Remember:

1. Rejection is not failure; it is redirection to where God wants us.
2. Don't be afraid of failing at something. Life is about trying new things.
3. Feelings aren't a good guide. Look to God for his truth in every situation.
4. God calls us to be faithful, not perfect.
5. When we're in the middle of a hard time, we need to remember to think back on all the ways God has been faithful in our lives and know he will be faithful again.

Three Questions to Ask:

1. Where have you felt rejected? In a relationship or at a specific place? Can you see where God might be using that to redirect you to something else?

2. Are there times when you don't try something or move on to a new thing because you are afraid of failure?

3. What seasons of your life can you look back on now and see God's goodness and faithfulness even when life felt hard?

Day 22

BE THE SALT AND THE LIGHT

MATTHEW 5:13a

Let me tell you why you are here. You're here to be salt-seasoning that brings out the God-flavors of this earth. (MSG)

I've always thought the analogy of God's people being the salt of the earth was really interesting, but I never quite understood it. But as I've gotten older, I've begun to see why God referred to us as salt.

So, what exactly does it mean?

In a literal sense, salt can be used to preserve food, like meats and vegetables. It enhances flavor. And it can be used to purify. Also, salt can be used to soothe sore muscles in a bath. I even think about when I've had cuts and went to the beach. There were times when I would have terrible turf burns from soccer and then put them in saltwater. It definitely stung for a second, but afterward there was relief, and by the end of the beach day, my cuts felt a lot better.

So we know salt can do all of those things, and we are told that we are "salt-seasoning that brings out the God-flavors of this earth." But how do we apply this practically to our lives?

If we are the seasoning, we are supposed to complement the "God-flavors of this earth"—that means that wherever we go, our lives should enhance others' perception of God. We should live in a way that will bring glory to him and let those around us see God in us. There are people in your life who may never go to church or a Bible study with you, but you can show them Jesus by loving them the way he loves us.

When we talk about bringing glory to God, we usually assume it has to be this big, extravagant accomplishment that is worthy of God's glory, when the reality is that being the salt looks more like showing up for the mundane day-to-day routine. It's going to practice, walking the halls at your school, or waking up early for work. It's looking for ways to enhance the lives of the people around you by loving them and finding areas where you can make a difference in their life. Sometimes that can be as simple as listening to a friend who's going through a hard time or befriending the new kid at school who has no one to sit with at lunch. Just like salt adds flavor to even the blandest food, we can add joy and love to the lives of people God puts before us by showing them his mercy and grace.

We can add joy and love to the lives of people God puts before us.

Day 23

STAY SALTY

MATTHEW 5:13b

If you lose your saltiness, how will people taste godliness? You've lost your usefulness and will end up in the garbage. (MSG)

People might call a few of us a little salty rather than sweet. I will own that and take it as a compliment. Sometimes I'm not the sweetest or most-liked person in the room, but I get things done and I'm true to myself. I hope a few of y'all reading this can relate to that a little bit.

Speaking the truth can be abrasive and intimidating to some. I think about the years I spent playing soccer. When I had a leadership role, I wanted us to do well as a team. In order to succeed, we had to give 110% to that goal. There were girls on my team I knew could absolutely give more. I could see their potential and, in a respectful way, I would call them out and push them harder.

Some of my teammates respected this quality in me and appreciated that I wanted them to play better. Others did not like it at all. They made fun of me behind my back, called me a try hard, and would not invite me to the big parties they threw.

Yeah, super fun, I loved it. Felt great.

But those girls who did appreciate my saltiness challenged each other and me, and we made each other faster and stronger. We succeeded and worked well on the field because we brought out the best in each other. In the same way, salt can initially irritate a wound but make it better in the long run.

When you are like salt, you will irritate some people, and often you won't be the most popular in the groups around you. Despite that, I want to encourage you to keep being like salt, even if it means sacrificing popularity—because this verse does ring true. If you lose that saltiness, how will people get to know God through you? When you aren't true to yourself and to God, you lose your impact and usefulness. So, own the saltiness and speak the truth, show others God in this way, and remain useful to the plans he has for you.

Own the saltiness and speak the truth, show others God in this way, and remain useful to the plans he has for you.

Day 24

GOD SEES YOU

GENESIS 16:13

She gave this name to the Lord who spoke to her: "You are the God who sees me," for she said, "I have now seen the One who sees me." (NIV)

I've heard people say that girls have gotten meaner, but the sad truth is women have been cruel to each other since the beginning of time.

One of the first examples is the relationship between Sarai and Hagar in Genesis 16. Sarai, the wife of Abram, is unable to have children, but God promises that one day she and Abram will have as many descendants as there are stars in the sky (see Gen. 15:5). Like so many of us, Sarai gets tired of waiting. So she and Abram take matters into their own hands (this always works out well), and Sarai brings in her servant, Hagar, to have a child with Abram. Hagar becomes pregnant and then Sarai gets jealous and mistreats Hagar to the point that Hagar runs away. Maybe there have been times that you've wished you could do that same thing while being mistreated. I know I have.

Now, Hagar is pregnant and alone, and it's there, at her lowest point in the wilderness, that an angel appears and says:

> You are now pregnant
>   and you will give birth to a son.
> You shall name him Ishmael,
>   for the Lord has heard of your misery. (v. 11 NIV)

After this happens, Hagar calls the Lord "El-roi" or "the God who sees me."

We are all really good at hiding when we are hurt. We hide behind makeup that conceals a red, splotchy face, or we keep our emotions together until we reach our car, then have a breakdown. We weep behind closed doors, wondering why we got overlooked again. Each one of us can think of a time when we felt utterly unnoticed in our sacrifices, work, struggle, and pain.

But like Hagar, we have a God who sees us.

Not only does he see us but he appreciates our sacrifice and toil, and he acknowledges it.

We have a God who sees us.

He holds every tear we have shed in the palm of his hand. He carries our pain and hurt just like it's his own. So the next time you are overlooked, forgotten, mistreated, or hiding away in the hurt, remember the story of Hagar, who went from crying alone in the wilderness to knowing God truly saw her pain and met her in it. God sees your trouble. He sees the losses you have experienced and knows the hurt you feel. He hears your prayers. So take heart in the fact that you have a God who is collecting the tears you've shed in the hidden moments, and he sees you even when you feel forgotten and overlooked. Others may reject you, betray you, or leave you out, but God never will.

God carries our pain and hurt just like it's his own.

Day 25

WHEN YOU DON'T FEEL IT

1 CORINTHIANS 2:1, 3

When I came to you, brothers and sisters, announcing the mystery of God to you, I did not come with brilliance of speech or wisdom. . . . I came to you in weakness, in fear, and in much trembling.

I was watching the TV series *The Chosen* the other night, and a specific line really stuck with me. In the episode, Jesus sends off his disciples to do mission work and he tells them that they now have the authority to perform miracles in God's name. Of course, like anyone who has just been told they can make the blind see and can cast out demons, they are in a little shock. Then Nathaniel, a disciple who is known for his honesty, says, "Well, I don't feel any different." Jesus looks him in the eye and says, "I don't need you to feel anything to do great things."*

We sometimes live under the impression that when doing the work of God, we should feel empowered, invincible, and unafraid,

* *The Chosen*, season 3, episode 2, "Two by Two," directed by Dallas Jenkins, written by Dallas Jenkins, Tyler Thompson, and Ryan Swanson, aired March 12, 2023, on TBN Films.

though never once has it been promised to us that our feelings will change the moment God calls us to something. I know for me, the moment God calls me to something, I feel even more unworthy, unequipped, and nervous than I was to begin with. I'm here to tell you that these feelings are completely normal. We are only human.

Even Paul, who was a revolutionary in the church, says he came "in weakness, in fear, and in much trembling" (1 Cor. 2:3). Noah was drunk, Moses had a stutter, Jeremiah was only a teenager, David had an affair, Thomas doubted, Peter had a temper, Elijah was depressed . . . I mean, the list goes on and on. Each one of these people, when viewed through a human lens, was completely unqualified for the roles God had them play, yet each one of them did something so revolutionary it ended up in the Bible.

God does not need us to be worthy or to feel prepared when he calls us. He needs us only to be faithful and to believe that he will be complete when we are lacking. We aren't always going to feel like we can carry out the task God has for us, and maybe that's on purpose. God wants us to know that the only way we can do it is with him. You have the power of the Holy Spirit in you. You are still going to mess up, and you are still going to feel like you can't do what you've been called to sometimes, but the Spirit is inside of you and God is walking you through every step of his plan. So even when you feel unworthy or ill-equipped, sit with the humility, knowledge, and truth that Christ will give you everything you need to reach the places he leads you.

God does not need us to be worthy or to feel prepared when he calls us.

Day 26

DEALING WITH DISAPPOINTMENT

HEBREWS 12:28

Therefore, since we are receiving a kingdom that cannot be shaken, let us be thankful. By it, we may serve God acceptably, with reverence and awe.

It hurts when we have plans that completely fall through. Change is usually not welcome in our lives, especially when we had our hopes set on something else. I, for one, hate change. I'm pretty sure it's genetic because my mom tells me a story about when she was dating my dad. He got a new truck, and she started crying because she thought, *Well, if he wants a new truck then maybe he wants a new girlfriend.* So I really have an uphill battle on this whole accepting change thing. Maybe you do too.

I remember how it felt to lose a lot of friends in high school and even at points during college. It sucked. I felt so helpless and lonely. Everything was just a big, fat unknown. It would be so much easier during hard times if we knew exactly what God was doing. Then we

would know the crappy times are definitely worth it because of this promised thing that we will get later on.

Unfortunately, though, that's just not how life works.

We don't know what good things will come out of the bad, and we don't know when we'll finally see them.

But God has a bird's-eye view of the whole situation. Even when we lose friends, significant others, finances, family, and plans, God is still working. I can't tell you exactly why things can't go according to your plan, and nothing I say will necessarily make you feel better, but I can tell you God's children will receive an inheritance and a kingdom that can't be shaken. When our lives get shaken up, we can trust that the things that remain are what has been unshaken. We can put our hope in the unshakable things from God when everything else around us feels fragile.

We can lean in, knowing that his love, his protection, and his kingdom aren't going to fail us. No purpose he has for our lives can be moved or changed, even when it feels like things are falling apart. Everything else in this world will, at some point, let us down and feel broken, but God won't. That is his promise to us.

We can put our hope in the unshakable things from God when everything else around us feels fragile.

Day 27

THE DIFFERENCE BETWEEN MAKING AND KEEPING

HEBREWS 12:14–15

Pursue peace with everyone, and holiness—without it no one will see the Lord. Make sure that no one falls short of the grace of God and that no root of bitterness springs up, causing trouble and defiling many.

I believe our culture and this world have given us a false image of peace. We think peace can be achieved by always being calm and gentle. In my life there have been times when I have wondered, *If I was a little more calm or gentle, then maybe I wouldn't have lost a lot of my friendships. Maybe I should've been more gracious when someone hurt me or I should have relented on whatever stance I had that caused the conflict.* I have examined each falling-out I've had and can't help but wonder, *What if I am the problem?* I mean, the common denominator in all those lost relationships is me. But when I look at the belief I backed up or the stance I took, I stand by it to this day because I know it was the truth.

God purposely put me in situations to see something or to call something out. While it sometimes led to conflict, he gave me the eyes to see, so I need to have the mouth to speak as well. Now, before I say anything further, I want you to understand I am not saying I'm totally in the right. I am human and sometimes things are more complicated than just right and wrong. But in those situations where I experienced conflict, I stood for what I believed and I didn't just roll over or avoid something for the sake of cultural "peace."

What I have realized is that our God is a God of truth. His real peace will never be achieved through ignoring a lie or disagreement and not confronting it. Striving for peace is not avoiding the conflict but dealing with it. When walking the straight path, you don't go around the obstacles but go through the conflict. We want true peace and sometimes the only way to achieve that is through addressing the conflict head-on. Matthew 5:9 says, "Blessed are the peacemakers, for they will be called children of God" (NIV). Making peace is not easy; if it was, then everyone wouldn't be striving so hard to achieve it.

There is a difference between being a peacekeeper and being a peacemaker. A peacekeeper tries to maintain a version of peace, sometimes avoiding conflict altogether for the sake of cultural peace. A peacemaker creates peace by facing the conflict head-on to find that godly peace. A peacemaker recognizes that you can't sacrifice the truth to avoid conflict because we are called to speak the truth in love.

A peacemaker creates peace by facing the conflict head-on to find that godly peace.

THE WEEKLY RECAP

Five Truths to Remember:

1. We can add joy to people's lives when we show them God's mercy and grace.
2. When we aren't true to who God created us to be, we lose our impact.
3. Others may reject, betray, or overlook us, but God never will.
4. No purpose that God has for our lives can be changed, even if things feel like they are falling apart.
5. God's peace will never be achieved through allowing a lie or disagreement to remain.

Three Questions to Ask:

1. Where can you show someone God's mercy and grace right now?

2. What are the places in your life where you need to believe that God has not overlooked you or forgotten you?

3. Is there a lie or disagreement right now that you believe God is asking you to confront and make right?

Day 29

FOCUSING ON WHAT REALLY MATTERS

PROVERBS 31:30

Charm is deceptive and beauty is fleeting,
but a woman who fears the Lord will be praised.

We can spend a lot of time thinking about our appearance. It's so easy to pick ourselves apart in the mirror and point out every little flaw that we see. I know I can sit and think about that one comment some guy in middle school made about my nose or wonder if the body I'm seeing in the mirror is *actually* what my body looks like or if what I see is a figment of my imagination created by all the little insecurities I have. We poke and prod at all the parts of ourselves we have no control over. We compare our worst features to the perfect, photoshopped version of someone else's best. And when we do this, our bodies and our features always come up short. They will never be the best in the room, and they will never be good enough for us.

The ideal image of ourselves is deceptive. It's a lie Satan throws in our face to distract us from all the other incredible things we have

going on. Hair color comes and goes, clothing sizes ebb and flow, and stretch marks are as normal as the sun rising every day. But the plans God has for us are forever. Showing Christ to someone has an eternal impact.

Ultimately, beauty is fleeting and won't last forever. The impact we have in this world does not come down to how good we look. It's the truth we speak, the way we love, and our fear of the Lord that last. Our bodies show our lives and what we have been through. Our bodies are a testimony of our adventures and our struggles. It is not easy to see ourselves through God's eyes, but when we read the way God speaks about women, we see that he finds us beautiful. He created mountains, sunsets, oceans, and still called us the thing that was "very good."

That doesn't mean insecurities are easy to handle. We will not always feel beautiful, but we can give ourselves perspective when we start feeling insecure. Beauty and looks come and go, but the way we care for others and the way God cares for us are everlasting.

Beauty and looks come and go, but the way we care for others and the way God cares for us are everlasting.

Day 30

HOPE IN THE HEARTBREAK

ROMANS 15:13

Now may the God of hope fill you with all joy and peace as you believe so that you may overflow with hope by the power of the Holy Spirit.

I never thought that I would look back with nostalgia to the day my heart was broken, but here I am thinking about it as I laugh at my computer screen. The day my breakup happened, I was kind of in shock. Half of me felt liberated, like a weight had been lifted off my shoulders, but the other half felt really let down and hurt. There were a few people I texted immediately to let them know, and each of them brought a level of love and encouragement that I will forever be grateful for, but the person I'm specifically thinking of today is my best friend Lyndi, who was also my roommate at the time.

I was sitting on my bed, processing everything that had just happened, when she burst into my room. Her hands were full with bags from Target. She had gotten me a fuzzy blanket, a candle, and some chocolate-covered blueberries. So basically all the necessities I needed to cope. She talked through things with me, and then the movie *The Proposal* somehow came up. She was absolutely horrified

that I hadn't seen it and dragged me out to the couch so we could watch it. And there we were. The day my heart had been broken, giggling at Ryan Reynolds.

We talked all about what we wanted in a guy, and she asked me what I dreamed of. What I realize now is that she was giving me hope. There was nothing she could've said to comfort me, no Scripture that would automatically fix my broken heart. But Lyndi gave me companionship and provided me with hope, anticipation, and excitement for what was to come.

Never underestimate the power of hope. Hebrews 6:18 calls us "to seize the hope set before us." Verse 19 says, "We have this hope as an anchor for the soul, firm and secure. It enters the inner sanctuary behind the curtain." Hope is one of the greatest gifts. Sometimes the greatest thing God can give us in hard moments is his companionship and hope for something better. The desires he gives us and the hope he provides are not meaningless or empty. He knows the plans he has for us. So in the hard times, have the hope for more and remember that God has plans bigger than whatever you can dream of. Our hope is knowing he is always working for our good, even when life seems painful.

The desires God gives us and the hope he provides are not meaningless or empty. He knows the plans he has for us.

Day 31

BUILDING SOMETHING THAT LASTS

ISAIAH 28:16

Therefore the Lord God said:
"Look, I have laid a stone in Zion,
a tested stone,
a precious cornerstone, a sure foundation;
the one who believes will be unshakable."

I am an extremely impatient person, and I have been my whole life. I like immediate results and love to be in control of the narrative in my life. Or, at least, I think that would be a good idea, though it would probably end in a dumpster fire. I'm guessing seasons of waiting are one of your least-favorite things as well.

Whether you're waiting to hear back from a college, waiting for loyal friends to come along, or waiting for a season of singleness to end, it is so hard living in a state where you're not quite sure what or when something is going to happen. There's a level of uneasiness and uncertainty that, for me, can lead to some anxiety. It's hard to

rationalize your feelings, and sometimes it can feel like time is running out or "it" absolutely has to happen soon.

You see people around you getting exactly what you're dreaming of, and it feels so unfair. But these seasons cause our faith to stretch. We are pushed and pulled by our surroundings, even as we serve an unshakable God. Our God is all-knowing and all-seeing. He sees the full plan he has for us and isn't going to let us settle for less because someone else's plan looks so much more appealing in that moment. The key word is *that*.

In a season of waiting, it seems it would be easier to settle for what you can immediately see, but that is less than what God has for you. I promise, when you look back at the end of the waiting period, you aren't going to wish for a different plan or story because the one that you experienced was perfect for you and your life.

I know this doesn't make it all better. It is really hard when your faith is being stretched daily. I like this verse in Isaiah because it talks about a "tested stone." This was a stone that was chosen to be part of the foundation of a building, but before it could be included, it had to be tested and proven. In that same way, our faith is supposed to be our foundation, but how can it support us if it's never been tested or proven reliable?

These waiting seasons build a level of resolve in us. We have to trust that God will bring the right thing in at the right time, and in this season of waiting, we still put our faith in motion. That is how God builds faith in our hearts that is unshakable.

We have to trust that God will bring the right thing in at the right time.

Day 32

GOD WANTS US TO TALK TO HIM

EXODUS 4:10

Moses said to the LORD, "Pardon your servant, Lord. I have never been eloquent, neither in the past nor since you have spoken to your servant. I am slow of speech and tongue." (NIV)

Sometimes when I pray, I feel this pressure to have the perfect words. I want to make sure that I am eloquent so that God can really get the meaning behind my words. I feel like when we hear people pray out loud, it can seem like their prayers are always so articulate and powerful and wrapped up so nicely. They get their exact point across. It's respectful and seems like the precise thing God wants to hear. It can make me feel less than or like I don't have enough experience to say a "really good" prayer when the reality is that the biggest requirement for a good prayer is to let the Lord hear your heart.

Each of us is going to pray differently, and no two prayers are going to sound the same, but that's the beauty of it. God just wants us to come to him with our fears, our worries, and our requests.

The whole point of prayer is to deepen our relationship with him. It's the gift of getting to have a conversation with the God who put the stars in the sky.

Often there are no words to express what we're feeling. There may be times in our lives when the only prayer we can offer is our tears or a heavy sigh. God already knows what we need, and he has a plan set in place for us before we ever come to him. All he asks is that we surrender our worries, our frustrations, our longings, and our hurts.

We don't have to say the right thing to God to have him solve our problem because he already knows the solution. All we have to do is go to God in the first place. He values our honesty and our vulnerability. There is no point in trying to hide or rationalize feelings before him because he already knows it all. He isn't afraid of our questions, our doubts, or our honesty.

I think about the story of Job and how he prayed throughout his struggles. He didn't just pray with praise. He was angry and frustrated. He wept and wrestled with God. He was honest about the state of his heart and yet never turned from God, even in his most resentful moments. That is honest prayer. It is so easy to get in the habit of overthinking our prayer life, but what God wants is not our eloquence but our hearts.

We don't have to say the right thing to God to have him solve our problem because he already knows the solution.

Day 33

HEALTHY GROWTH REQUIRES PRUNING

JOHN 15:1–2

I am the true vine, and my Father is the gardener. He cuts off every branch in me that bears no fruit, while every branch that does bear fruit he prunes so that it will be even more fruitful. (NIV)

A few months ago, I decided to invest in a real plant for my bedroom. I realized I was in no position to get a pet, and I had no clue if I could take care of another living thing besides myself—some nights I would forget to feed myself dinner—so a plant felt like a great test case.

I fully prepared myself that this poor plant, which I named Lewis, would have a short and tragic life. However, I'm proud to report that Lewis is still alive. He is weirdly thriving. I don't know if it's because I water him with the leftovers from my gym bottle, which has a little pre-workout powder mixed in, or if it's because of God's grace. He knows that Lewis's death might be too much of an emotional hit for me right now.

Now that Lewis is growing, I'm learning how to prune him. Pruning seems so counterintuitive to growth. This plant has worked so hard to grow new leaves and vines, and now I just have to chop them off and make poor Lewis start again.

As I've been in a season that requires a lot of growing and changing, this plant has become pretty symbolic for me. For example, when I got it, the first thing I did was dig it up, clean up its roots, then repot the whole thing. Funny enough, when God wants to grow us, he usually puts us in a new environment as well. He unbinds our tangled past, then gives us the space we need to stretch out. Whether that's a loss of a friend group, a relationship, or us truly moving somewhere new, it means it's time for us to stretch out. We have a new space to grow. Instead of looking at change as a loss, we can choose to see the challenge for growth in it.

Growth is never going to be perfectly linear. There will be ups and downs and some hard lessons to learn. But let's not focus on the missteps as "regression," but rather as refining. God is shaping you. He wants the growth that occurs to be healthy. While these changes can hurt and feel discouraging or like a loss, all we have to do in these moments is shift our perspective.

God is shaping you and pruning you to thrive. This process isn't always the easiest, and there are times it doesn't seem to make sense, but trust his process and know that he is moving you to new places where you can continue to grow in a healthy way.

God is shaping you and pruning you to thrive.

Day 34

FORGIVING WHEN IT'S HARD TO FORGIVE

1 JOHN 4:20

If anyone boasts, "I love God," and goes right on hating his brother or sister, thinking nothing of it, he is a liar. (MSG)

When someone hurts me or when I feel betrayed, it's really easy to forget about the whole "love thy enemy" verse in the Bible, and it's a lot easier to think about the "let him rain burning coals and sulfur on the wicked; let a scorching wind be the portion in their cup" verse (see Ps. 11:6). It feels more natural to me.

After a falling out, I can get in a bad habit of dehumanizing the person I am fighting. I love the fact that God loves and cares for me and will be with me through all of my pain, but I struggle with the idea that he'll do the exact same thing for others. I mean, one of us has to be in the right so it feels like God should just take care of the one in the right, right?

Incorrect. This is one of many reasons why I am not God.

Every single one of us is in the wrong. Yet Jesus still took all our punishment on himself. Even the sins of the one who hurt you.

Sometimes it's easy to think we deserve more than another person because of our good intentions and actions, but the reality is that, no matter what, we deserve nothing, yet we still get everything because of God's perfect love.

It's easy to forget the fact that Jesus is working on the ones who have wronged us in the same way he is working on us. We try to place our human emotions on him and, of course, we don't understand and, of course, we can't forgive from this perspective. We are broken people living in a broken world. But this is where we are called to be not of this earth. We have to apply a godly view to our hurt and to our emotions. We need to see the perfect love Christ has for us and know that we have no right to hold resentment in our hearts toward someone else. The forgiveness we are called to have for others might not always come in the form of a feeling, because our feelings can be deceiving. Instead, it's willpower.

We have to trust that God sees all and knows all and let go of the pain from the past. When we choose to hold on to unforgiveness, we are ultimately hurting only ourselves. This isn't always easy, but because Christ loved us first, we are now called to love those around us in the same way. Let go and rest in the knowledge that God is working on the heart of the person you are struggling to forgive.

Let go and rest in the knowledge that God is working on the heart of the person you are struggling to forgive.

THE WEEKLY RECAP

Five Truths to Remember:

1. Beauty and looks come and go. Our heart and our character are what matter to God.
2. The desires God has for us are bigger than we can imagine, and we can trust him amid heartbreak.
3. We shouldn't settle for what we can see in front of us because God usually has something better in mind that we can't see yet.
4. Faith can be our strong foundation only after it's been proven and tested.
5. God is working on the hearts of people we may be struggling to forgive.

Three Questions to Ask:

1. Am I too focused on my outward appearance and not paying enough attention to my heart and my character?

2. Are there places in my life where I am settling for less than what God has for me because I'm afraid of the unknown and the unseen?

3. Is there someone God is calling me to forgive and trust that he is working on their heart?

Day 36

INFORMATION OVERLOAD

ISAIAH 54:17

No weapon formed against you will succeed,
and you will refute any accusation
raised against you in court.
This is the heritage of the LORD's servants,
and their vindication is from me.

We have grown up in a world fairly different from our parents'. Ours is louder and faster-paced, and everything we ever want to know is at our fingertips. Yet our generation is the most anxious ever. I have to believe so much of it is because, at the tap of a screen, we see everything we wish we were—or even the horrific wreckage in a war-torn country. We are constantly exposed to things we were never meant to see or process at this magnitude.

People can now hide behind a screen and say whatever they want to tear you down. Proverbs 18:21 says, "Death and life are in the power of the tongue," and someone can speak (or type) those words with zero forethought or consequences now. It is so easy to become discouraged, to be afraid, and to experience anxiety with everything we are exposed to on a daily basis.

There is an immense amount of pressure on us to behave a certain way. And it may seem like our phones give people a certain power over us and we have the same power over them. It can feel like a force we can never really escape because it follows us around on a tiny screen.

This so-called pressure or power is just an illusion. We believe this idea that people can mess up God's plan for us through something they might say or do to us. We worry that if someone says the right mean thing or spreads rumors to the right person, then our reputation is finished. We forget that we belong to the King Most High and that the things of this world have absolutely no power over us.

What I have realized is that people have as much power and control over us as we give them. If you have the perspective that a person can hurt you, then they can and probably will. But if you shift that perspective and realize that you are a daughter of the Almighty, then what on earth could people do to bring harm to you? Your plans and your inheritance are secure in Christ so hold fast to him and to his truth, and don't believe the lies being thrown your way.

Your plans and your inheritance are secure in Christ so hold fast to him and to his truth.

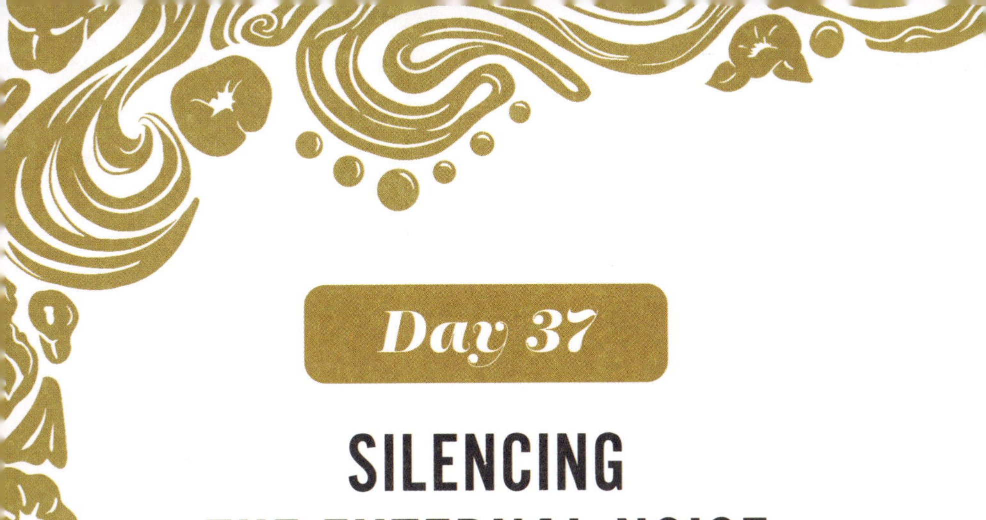

Day 37

SILENCING THE EXTERNAL NOISE

ZEPHANIAH 3:17

The Lord your God is with you,
the Mighty Warrior who saves.
He will take great delight in you;
in his love he will no longer rebuke you,
but will rejoice over you with singing. (NIV)

We live in a time when we expect instant gratification. The videos we watch are about fifteen seconds long, and if they're more, we get bored. We can watch a whole season of our favorite show in one day. If we choose to, we really never have to be alone with our thoughts. We can constantly put them off or drown them out in a whole manner of ways.

I think about times when I get anxious or upset and my reaction is to watch funny videos on my phone and not think about my feelings. There is nothing wrong with watching some funny videos to make you laugh during a hard time, but like all things, there needs to be balance and moderation. Something we have to keep in mind is that Satan's number one goal is to distance us from God. And there's no better way to do that than by surrounding us with the constant noise of the media. If Satan can use something to turn up that noise and we allow him to do that, how will our minds and hearts be quiet enough for us to tend to our soul with God?

When we get sucked into the noise, the voice of God's promises becomes quieter and quieter. Not because his voice is any less prominent but because we quit paying attention to it. Instead of turning to him, we drown out our feelings or worries by scrolling and then wonder why we don't feel any better.

We also tend to distance ourselves from God after we mess up. It's a natural instinct of the flesh. I mean, all you have to do is go back to Genesis to see that Adam and Eve's first instinct was to hide as well. And it's become easier to hide due to the sheer amount of distraction we have available to us.

God's Word says that no creature or thing "will be able to separate us from the love of God" (Rom. 8:39). Notice how it says the love of God. It doesn't say the wrath, disappointment, or discipline of God. It says love. Because at the end of the day, Satan loves to try to fill us with fear, shame, or guilt to keep us distant from God. This ensures that we choose distraction and hide from the confrontation when God is always ready to meet us with unconditional, undeniable love. So when you begin to feel shame or guilt, fight the instinct to hide and, instead, run toward God.

It's when we choose to sit in the stillness of his presence that we will experience his mercy and peace. Let his light drown out the lies of shame, anxiety, and guilt that he never meant for you to feel.

It's when we choose to sit in the stillness of God's presence that we will experience his mercy and peace.

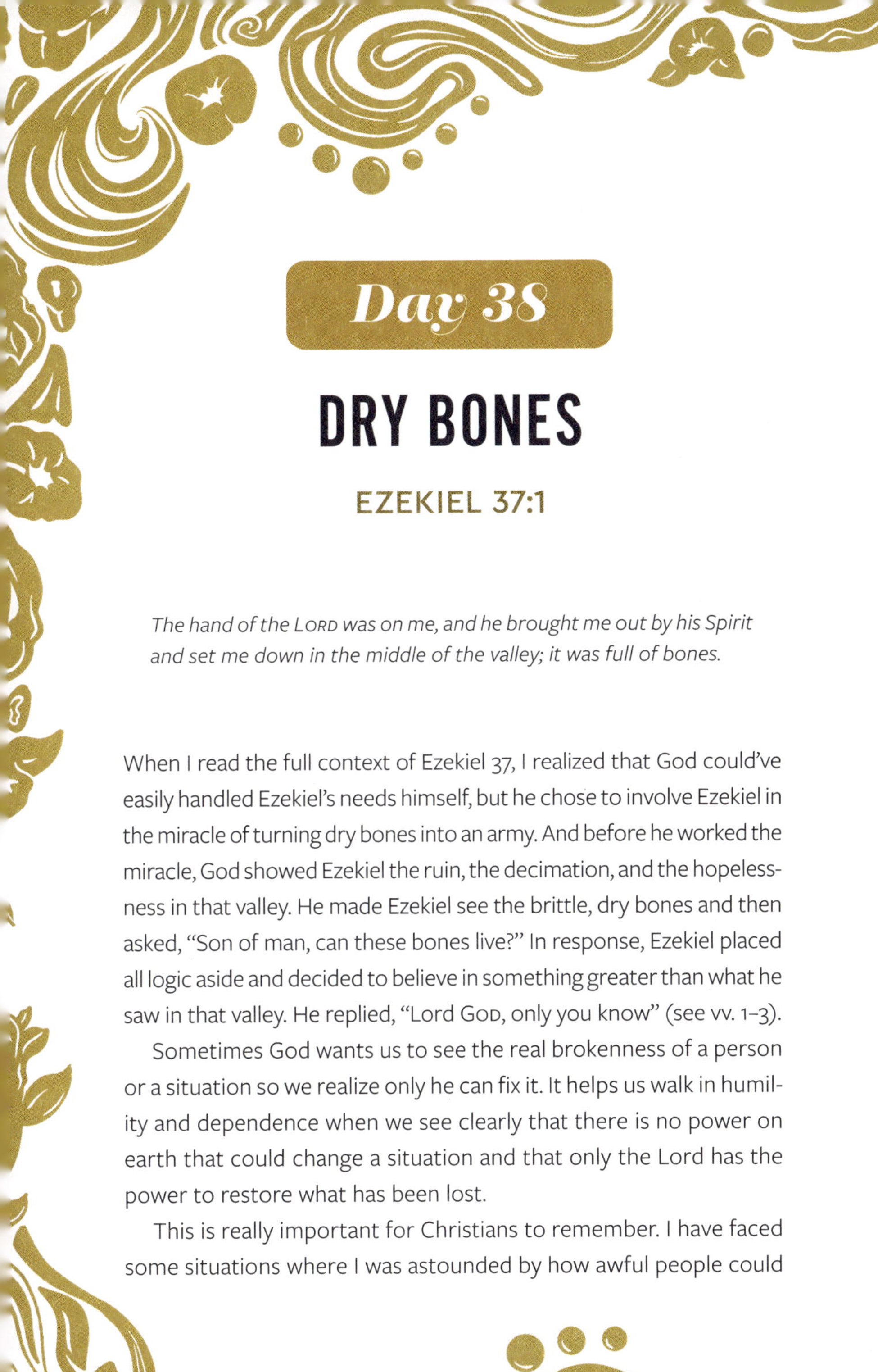

Day 38

DRY BONES

EZEKIEL 37:1

The hand of the Lord was on me, and he brought me out by his Spirit and set me down in the middle of the valley; it was full of bones.

When I read the full context of Ezekiel 37, I realized that God could've easily handled Ezekiel's needs himself, but he chose to involve Ezekiel in the miracle of turning dry bones into an army. And before he worked the miracle, God showed Ezekiel the ruin, the decimation, and the hopelessness in that valley. He made Ezekiel see the brittle, dry bones and then asked, "Son of man, can these bones live?" In response, Ezekiel placed all logic aside and decided to believe in something greater than what he saw in that valley. He replied, "Lord God, only you know" (see vv. 1–3).

Sometimes God wants us to see the real brokenness of a person or a situation so we realize only he can fix it. It helps us walk in humility and dependence when we see clearly that there is no power on earth that could change a situation and that only the Lord has the power to restore what has been lost.

This is really important for Christians to remember. I have faced some situations where I was astounded by how awful people could be. Things felt hopeless and bleak. But here's what I have learned: God shows us this brokenness so we know exactly where we are called to minister. He puts us in those dark valleys to draw out the response "Lord, only you" from our hearts.

The good news in Ezekiel is the story doesn't end with a valley of dry bones. God calls Ezekiel to prophesy the Word of the Lord, and as he speaks God's Word, those bones rattle and rise back to life to form a great army. Where moments before there had just been a desolate graveyard, now stands an army to deliver Israel because the powerful Word of the Lord has been faithfully spoken.

The same thing that happened in that desolate, barren place can happen in your life as well. In the hopeless moments or the hard situations, know that God placed you there for a purpose. He can work without you, but he chooses to use you to speak life and work miracles in his name.

Can you have that same faith and obedience in your valleys? Do you realize the power your voice, your life, and your ministry have over a bleak and hopeless future? All it takes is grit, faith, and obedience to speak out over those bones and believe that God can bring life and hope where all you see is destruction and death.

In the hopeless moments or the hard situations, know that God placed you there for a purpose.

Day 39

THE TRUTH IN LOVE

JOHN 15:19

If you were of the world, the world would love you as its own; but because you are not of the world, but I chose you out of the world, therefore the world hates you. (ESV)

Yesterday we discussed how God will sometimes bring us into desolate places so we can speak his Word and life over those in the midst of darkness. We talked about how God chooses to use us for his kingdom and how we need to have the faith and obedience to act. God is always calling us to speak truth to those around us, but let me be the first to say that it is not always easy.

When you realize that you need to speak up, like in a friend group that does not know God, among a group of girls who are excluding you, in a classroom with a professor trying to prove God isn't real, or wherever else it might be, it can be intimidating to take a bold step of faith. Also, it can be really hard to do it with love in your heart. Yet, the number one thing we are called to do in Christ is to love those around us.

I have a friend who doesn't believe in God, and one time he told me that "for a religion called to love unconditionally, Christians have

some of the most conditional love out there." He talked about how Christians will say they love you until they realize you aren't changing your beliefs, then they just cut you out or try to argue with you on why God is real.

Even in the hard times, we need to remember that we are daughters of the King, who will clothe us with strength in all circumstances and always uphold us. So even if I am struggling with friendships and have to fight even harder for the strength to speak up in the future, I know I can get through it. Not in my own power, but in his.

We cannot allow ourselves to be victims of this world because we are not of it, and there will be times the world will hate us precisely because of the God we love and serve. It will take grit, resilience, and faith to fight for our God and to choose the mindset that we won't fall into self-pity or victimhood. Ultimately, we serve someone greater than ourselves, and no matter our circumstance, we will be delivered. Even the worst stories can be used for good if we choose to keep our eyes on him.

Even the worst stories can be used for good if we choose to keep our eyes on God.

Day 40

THE LIE OF COMFORT

1 PETER 4:12–13

Dear friends, don't be surprised when the fiery ordeal comes among you to test you, as if something unusual were happening to you. Instead, rejoice as you share in the sufferings of Christ.

I think one of the biggest lies of modern Christianity is the idea that the Christian life promises we'll be comfortable. In believing that untruth, we have decided to make our God a god of comfort and convenience. Do you want to get that good grade or to win that game? Do you want that job promotion or to be accepted by that friend group? Well then, ask God.

I understand why this mindset is promoted. I mean, the promise of comfort and peace draws people into religion. But it's also the same thing that causes so many people to walk away in disappointment because it's confusing. They wonder, *If I serve such a good God, then why do bad things happen to me? Why am I struggling? Isn't that all supposed to go away?*

The honest answer is bad things will still happen because life is hard. You may even be more uncomfortable as a Christian at times

than you were before. We don't put our faith in God because he makes our life on this earth more comfortable. We put our faith in him because everything about him is greater than what our human minds can comprehend. There is so much more to our lives than the comfort and ease we see in the world. We are still going to be put through struggles. Just look at the stories in the Bible.

Daniel got thrown in the lions' den; David had to fight Goliath (then was on the run for years before becoming king); Shadrach, Meshach, and Abednego got thrown into the fire; and Joseph was falsely accused and spent time in prison. God does not take away the struggle; he delivers us from it. Without adversity, faith, grit, and resilience cannot be formed.

Each one of the stories I mentioned is powerful and significant. If God had just stopped all the bad things from happening, where would those people be? Where would the power of their testimonies come from? We are not called to live a comfortable life on earth because we are called higher. But take heart in the fact that every single one of these people was delivered. God allowed them to experience hard times, but in the end, they triumphed. The same can be said for our lives.

You will come out on the other side with the gift of knowing what God has done in your life. Your struggle becomes a powerful part of your story if you allow God to walk with you through it.

Your struggle becomes a powerful part of your story if you allow God to walk with you through it.

Day 41

THE TRUTH ABOUT FEELINGS

MATTHEW 14:28–29

"Lord, if it's you," Peter answered him, "command me to come to you on the water."

He said, "Come."

And climbing out of the boat, Peter started walking on the water and came toward Jesus.

Peter is one of my favorite disciples. I know I should say it's because of all he did for the gospel, but really it's because of his temper. Peter had strong emotions and a fiery temperament that I relate to and admire.

History tells us that Peter was crucified on an upside-down cross because he told his persecutors that he didn't deserve to die the same death as his Savior. He had a fiery faith in God, even in his last moments. But when put in a stressful situation, even Peter doubted and denied knowing his God. His emotions were one of his greatest strengths but also one of his greatest weaknesses.

I feel like a lot of us can relate to that. My mom likes to tell me that I have level 10 reactions to level 2 situations, and I hate to say it but she's not wrong.

We are often taught that our emotions are wrong, especially as girls. It's so easy for us to be seen as overly emotional or dramatic, but what we forget is that our God is emotional too. We were given our feelings and emotions for a purpose. They are a weapon that can be used to build up the kingdom or to tear us down. I believe this truth is painted clearly when Peter walks on water.

We know that he wasn't afraid of challenging everything and everyone around him. At this moment Peter decides to go big or go home by telling Jesus, "Lord, if it's you, command me to come to you on the water." Jesus calls him to come out and Peter does. He walks on water. He has the faith to step out of that boat. We see his emotions here, and they are strong. He challenges Jesus, he dares to walk on water, and the fighter in him pushes him to take that step of faith.

But in this moment, he also takes his eyes off Jesus and focuses on the storm around him. The emotions that were his greatest weapon at first become the thing that causes him to sink. How many times can this be said about us as well? The emotions we have are good, but only when our focus is on Jesus and what he says is true. When we take our eyes off Jesus and focus on the adversity around us, those same emotions begin to warp and become something of flesh and doubt. Your emotions are powerful and can lead to incredible moments of walking in faith and belief, but the only way to do that is to focus on Christ and keep our feelings and emotions in check.

Your emotions are powerful and can lead to incredible moments of walking in faith and belief.

Day 42

THE WEEKLY RECAP

Five Truths to Remember:

1. People have only as much power and control over us as we allow them to have.
2. When we feel shame or guilt, God wants us to run to him with it.
3. Sometimes God wants us to see the real brokenness of a person or a situation so we know that only he can fix it.
4. Even in the hard times, we need to remember that we are daughters of the King, who will clothe us with strength in all circumstances and always uphold us.
5. Our current struggles will become a powerful part of our story of God's faithfulness.

Three Questions to Ask:

1. How can you invite more quiet into your life so that you can hear God's voice more clearly?

2. Have you allowed shame and guilt over something you've done to distance you from God and his love for you?

3. What struggle are you facing that you need to trust that God can use for good?

Day 43

WALKING ON WATER

MATTHEW 14:30–31

Beginning to sink he cried out, "Lord, save me!"

Immediately Jesus reached out his hand, caught hold of him, and said to him, "You of little faith, why did you doubt?"

Even when we doubt, Jesus still catches us. I know I put so much pressure on myself to get "it" right, whatever "it" might be. A little voice in my head whispers that it's all up to me now and I better not screw things up. I start to believe that whatever happens next is a direct result of my efforts, whether good or bad. That little voice grows a mountain of anxiety, makes me overthink every social interaction I've ever had, causes me to fear the unknown, and plants seeds of doubt in my heart. It makes me want to try to control who or what I am, and as a result, it diminishes who God created me to be because I'm not surrendering all to him.

The truth is, we struggle to surrender all of ourselves because we know that not every part of us is good. We want to give our best to God but then hide the ugly stuff away. But when we put that pressure on ourselves, then that becomes our focus. Peter did the same thing when he focused on that storm and began to sink.

When Peter saw the wind and the waves around him, he was reminded of his humanity and how powerless he was standing out there in the middle of the sea. I know when I look at my mistakes and my failures, I have that same feeling. Like I'm sinking. Like once again I have messed up and this, of course, is the end.

But as Peter sank, he cried out "Lord, save me" and *immediately* Jesus reached out his hand and caught him. In the middle of Peter's doubt, the Lord caught him. In the middle of our doubt, God will catch us as well. God has never once said that it was all up to us. Satan will fill our head with lies that try to put our focus on the storm instead of Christ. We believe we have to hide the bad, but God wants all of us. Thorns, doubts, disbelief, and all. He doesn't want us to hide and fear the storm. He wants us to walk on water with him. And even when we fall short, he is there to catch us every single time. So let go, knowing that you will be caught, and be exactly who you are called to be in Christ.

So let go, knowing that you will be caught, and be exactly who you are called to be in Christ.

Day 44

THE BATTLE WE FACE

EPHESIANS 6:10–11

Finally, be strengthened by the Lord and by his vast strength. Put on the full armor of God so that you can stand against the schemes of the devil.

We often forget that every day when we wake up, we face a battle. If you are still alive and breathing, then it means that the breath in your lungs will be used in God's will to vanquish darkness. As I type this out, I feel like some of y'all may be like "Jeez, Caroline, I literally don't even have a driver's license yet. Calm down." And, yeah, fair enough, but don't let the significance of your life get lost on you. Don't downplay your own importance in God's plan.

At the end of our sophomore year of college, a good friend of mine met me for dinner. I hadn't seen her in a while because life had gotten busy, but the moment we started talking, I noticed an immediate difference in her. She was lighter and more joyful, so I asked her what had changed. She told me that she now had a real relationship with God and had found a peace she had never had before. Of course, I was so happy for her, but then she said something

I wasn't expecting. She looked at me and thanked me. Then she said, "You know you played a big part in that."

I have zero idea what I did. I don't remember saying anything truly profound to her, but apparently whatever I had said planted a seed in her heart that was able to flourish later on. Sometimes we think that to have an impact in the world, we have to have a major, dramatic moment when, really, the most dangerous thing we can do is wake up every day, know it's a battle, and put on the armor of God. We believe battles to be these tangible, physical experiences of blood, sweat, and tears. And while, yes, they can manifest as that, sometimes our biggest battles are spiritual.

The devil schemes and plots, and the more you try to abide in Christ, the harder you are going to get hit. But our Lord has vast strength and has given you the armor of truth, righteousness, peace, faith, salvation, and the Word of God. Each of us has battles that we are called to fight, both seen and unseen. You may never see the results of them or even know the true war that was waged, but each day, remember the Lord's strength and realize the significance of the role you play and that he has equipped you to fight every step of the way.

Remember the Lord's strength and realize the significance of the role you play and that he has equipped you to fight every step of the way.

Day 45

A LITTLE LIGHT MAKES A BIG DIFFERENCE

NEHEMIAH 8:10

This day is holy to our Lord. Do not grieve, for the joy of the Lord is your strength. (NIV)

I have this memory of my dad from when I was a little girl. We were talking about the spiritual world one night, and I had just discovered that demons were a real thing. I remember being really spooked, and at the time, it confirmed for me that there really were monsters under my bed. I told my dad I was scared, so he picked me up and started turning off all the lights in our house. Then he walked into the kitchen with me in his arms. I buried my face in his shoulder because I was frightened by all the darkness, but he told me to look up and look around the dark house. He asked if I could see the art in our living room or see anything else clearly. Of course I couldn't, and I was so fearful because the pitch-black house seemed so vast. But then he grabbed a lighter and lit the flame.

He asked me the same questions again, and this time I could actually see the house, and things were less scary because there was light. He looked at me and said, “A single flame just lit up this whole room. A little spark of light just overcame a house full of dark.” He told me that this is how our God works. Even a small sliver of faith (or light) will overpower the enemy’s darkness.

I can’t help but think about how many times we get scared of our own version of a dark house. We let our thoughts and worries run wild. Darkness and doubts can appear overpowering. It can hold our anxiety, insecurities, and doubt. But it’s just an illusion—a lie. A small flame can vanquish the darkness in a moment. It reminds me of Nehemiah 8:10 that says, “The joy of the Lord is your strength.” That joy is the small flame my dad held up in the dark house. That joy sends the enemy running and leaves him powerless. All we need is a small spark.

The joy and peace of God don’t come from a feeling but from the Creator of the universe. When we are surrounded by the lies of Satan that tell us to be overwhelmed or that we are not enough, we have to hold on to that light. That light is the truth of the power of God to defeat the darkness. He’s holding us, telling us to look up and see his truth, which will illuminate his power and drive away our doubts and fears.

Even a small sliver of faith (or light) will overpower the enemy’s darkness.

Day 46

OUR DEFINITION OF FAILURE AND SUCCESS

PHILIPPIANS 1:6

I am sure of this, that he who started a good work in you will carry it on to completion until the day of Christ Jesus.

One of my friends was feeling discouraged one day because she had just decided to drop her pursuit of her PhD. It became apparent it was a door that was closing, and she wasn't meant to go through it. She is a really driven person, so this decision was hard for her to make.

While we were talking, she said, "For the first time in my life I'm really failing and quitting something." But the reality is, in God's eyes this was absolutely not a failure. She spent three years on her PhD for a reason, and it may have not been to finally get "Dr." in her name. God had placed her there in that season for a purpose and then he also closed that door for a purpose, even if it doesn't make sense to her right now.

We can get in the bad habit of judging our failures and successes by the wrong standards. We think if something looks good on paper

or to others then it must be a success, but if it doesn't, we decide it's a failure. We can look at a door that closed "too soon" as a failure and miss the bigger picture. What we need to remember is that when God has a plan and starts something in you, he will carry it on to completion. If it is God's will for you, then its purpose will be fulfilled.

God will put us in situations for a lot more reasons than just to add something to a résumé. Our passions and dreams usually place us in circumstances that God manufactured for his glory. He uses each moment to teach us something. We look at success as what we accomplish in the world, but what about what we accomplish for the kingdom of heaven? The lives we impact, the experiences we learn from, or the people we meet who became close friends.

So when a door closes or something looks different than you thought it would, don't look at it as a mistake or a loss; instead, realize that the moment has served its purpose. You have learned and loved exactly as you were supposed to. Be confident that the good work that was started will be seen all the way to the end. Success in God's economy usually looks very different from what the world focuses on. Don't be afraid of failure, because it is sometimes the very thing God is using to get you where he wants you to be.

Success in God's economy usually looks very different from what the world focuses on.

Day 47

YOU ARE NOT A VICTIM

PSALM 18:35–36

You have given me the shield of your salvation;
your right hand upholds me,
and your humility exalts me.
You make a spacious place beneath me for my steps,
and my ankles do not give way.

Sometimes we can fall into a trap of self-pity. When things don't go according to our plan or something bad happens, we feel sorry for ourselves or like we're a powerless victim. But when we have this mentality, even if we don't realize it, we are discounting God's power and his plan for us.

At the end of my sophomore year of high school, I attended a banquet for my soccer team. Each year at the banquet the new captains were announced. I was really expecting to be named to that position—I had been a starter all year and had taken a leadership role on the team.

During the banquet the coach announced a different girl as captain, and it still makes me feel sick, even as I write about this years later. Everyone clapped and then turned to see my reaction. I was

excited for the girl who was picked, but I couldn't help feeling like I had been robbed. It felt so unfair, and I was totally blindsided. Even my teammates recognized that, which made it more embarrassing for me. After everything I had already faced that year, I felt like I was due for a win.

Here's what I realized as I processed the situation: I am not a victim of my circumstances. What happened to me might have been unfair and I had every right to be upset, but I needed to shift my focus. Even in the hurt, I chose to focus on the fact that the God I serve is just. We will often have seasons where we take hit after hit, but we serve a victorious God who is always working all things for our good.

Even in the hard times, we need to remember we are daughters of the King and that he will deliver us to spacious places. So even when we struggle, we can rest knowing that we can get through things—not in our own power, but in his.

We cannot allow ourselves to be victims of this world because we are not of it. There will be times the world will hate us precisely because of the God we love and serve. He is always building something better in us than what we are able to see in the moment.

Remember we are daughters of the King and that he will deliver us to spacious places.

Day 48

FAILURE TO FAITH

JAMES 4:10

Humble yourselves before the Lord, and he will exalt you.

Whenever I am struggling—whether it's with life, sin, hurt, or loss—my tendency is to do everything in my power to get through it. I want to be strong and able to just push through. It can feel like a failure if I can't get over something or if I let my circumstance impact me negatively, but what I often forget is that I was never created to go through adversity in my own power. This has been—and maybe still is—a little bit of a pride issue. I want to be able to stand on my own and deal with whatever adversity comes my way in my own strength, but that isn't how God created his people.

We need him as we face all the challenges and disappointments that life brings. None of us are strong enough to fight battles ourselves. In order to push through hard seasons, we have to humble ourselves before God. The bravest, strongest thing we can do is admit that we can't face life alone. We have to cry out and say that we need help and then give God room to work. We need to surrender it all to him.

At church recently my pastor said, "The power of God shall raise us up the moment we bow down."* This is one of the truest things I have heard. We see our failures, disappointments, and shortcomings and if we can't overcome them, then we view it as a failure. But God wants us to trade that failure for faith. We don't have to get it right every time, and we don't have to always try to control the outcome. All we have to do is surrender and have faith that our God will equip us and support us through anything. He wants us to lean on him. He desires our dependence because he wants us to have a real relationship with him, and he wants to work through us.

So, yes, we will be put in positions and through difficulties that we cannot handle on our own—maybe that's where you are today—but God will use each moment to train us and prepare us for what's ahead. So don't try to handle it on your own. Let go of the pressure and stress of your situation and trust that God has got you. Instead of looking at your struggle, keep your eyes on him and have faith that his grace will uphold you.

Let go of the pressure and stress of your situation and trust that God has got you.

---

* Jonathan Brooks, "'Who All' Experiences God," at Restoration Church on July 28, 2024.

Day 49

THE WEEKLY RECAP

Five Truths to Remember:

1. In the middle of our doubts, God is there to catch us.
2. God has equipped us to fight every battle we face.
3. When we are surrounded by the dark lies of the enemy that tell us to be overwhelmed or that we are not enough, we have to hold on to God's light.
4. Success in God's eyes often looks very different from what the world focuses on.
5. We are never helpless victims of our circumstances because God will always use even our hardest times for our good when we keep our focus on him.

Three Questions to Ask:

1. Where are you focused on the darkness in your life instead of on allowing God's light to shine truth on the situation?

2. Are there places where you are acting like a victim instead of trusting that God can use this hard time for good?

3. Are you more focused on what the world calls success than the things that God considers success?

Day 50

SEEING OTHERS AS GOD DOES

COLOSSIANS 3:12–13

Therefore, as God's chosen ones, holy and dearly loved, put on compassion, kindness, humility, gentleness, and patience, bearing with one another and forgiving one another if anyone has a grievance against another.

All of us can be guilty of being quick to decide something about a person that may not be true, based only on what we see on the outside. We see a girl we know on social media whose life looks so perfect that we can't decide whether we kind of hate her, want to be like her, or just want to unfollow her. We think her life is amazing based on a few random photographs that have been perfectly filtered and captioned when the truth is we have no idea what she may be wrestling with on the inside.

All of us have challenges, struggles, anxieties, and insecurities that we have learned to keep buried deep inside, and I think it's easy to forget that we aren't the only ones who do this. Everyone we meet is dealing with their own problems, even if we can't see them on the surface.

There have been several times when I've assumed the worst about a person or taken something they've said or done personally, when their actions weren't about me at all. During high school I had a friend who would sometimes catch me off guard with a rude comment about my appearance, and it never felt great. But after spending more time with her family, I realized this was the way her mom treated her. She lived in a family where the whole focus was on her outward appearance, and I began to understand that one of the ways she coped with this was to pick other girls apart the same way her mother picked her apart. I'm not saying that her behavior was okay, but seeing the depth of what she was struggling with gave me compassion and understanding that I didn't have before.

We never know what someone else is dealing with, and we will never regret treating someone with compassion and kindness, even if there are times we don't feel like they deserve it. It doesn't mean that we should excuse bad behavior; rather, we are learning to love others the way Jesus loves us. None of us are going to get this right every time, but it's good to remember that before we jump to conclusions about a person, we should take a minute to ask God to give us the grace to view them the way he does.

We will never regret treating someone with compassion and kindness.

Day 51

HE IS WHO HE SAYS HE IS

JOB 42:5

I had heard reports about you,
but now my eyes have seen you.

If you need to put your hard time into perspective, I recommend reading the book of Job. I will warn you, it is not a feel-good tale. Job experienced devastation and losses that most of us can't even imagine.

However, reading his story might help you realize things could be much worse than not making the team or being left out by your friends on a Friday night. Neither of those things is easy, but they are significantly better than what Job lived through. We will all have hard times in life and things that don't turn out the way we hoped or planned. I'm only twenty-one, and I've already dealt with disappointments and hurts that have tested my faith and made me question God.

But what I love about the story of Job is how he holds on to his faith in God despite everything around him being terrible. Even his wife encourages him to just curse God and die after all that he has

been through. But Job continues to trust God and doesn't let his circumstances change that trust. Moreover, he is honest with God. He weeps, laments, and is vulnerable about his true struggles with God. He doesn't just act like it's all fine.

When I look back at seasons that were filled with being left out, having people say terrible things about me, painful heartbreak, and feelings of loneliness, I can see how those were the very times when my faith grew the most because I had to really decide if I believed that God is who he says he is. As we grow up, it's not enough for us to believe in God because our parents do or because of what we learned in church or because we had a great time this summer at church camp.

Real, deep faith comes when we go through hard times that cause us to truly see God for ourselves. This is the kind of faith that will sustain us for the rest of our lives, no matter what comes our way. Later in Job's life, God gives him even more than what he originally lost. It's when we see the way God loves us and comforts us during the most challenging times in our life that we are encouraged. Those moments push our faith and make us stronger.

Real, deep faith comes when we go through hard times that cause us to truly see God for ourselves.

Day 52

OWN YOUR GIFTS

1 CORINTHIANS 12:14, 17, 18

Indeed, the body is not one part but many. . . . If the whole body were an eye, where would the hearing be? . . . God has arranged each one of the parts in the body just as he wanted.

I have always loved watching the Olympics because we not only get to see all these talented athletes make history but we also get to see them support each other under one flag. They all have completely different skills but one common goal—to win and lift each other up while competing. I feel like this is a good example of how we should act as believers in the church and as women of God.

We can get so caught up in the game of comparison. It's what ends so many female friendships, causes so many arguments, and leads to lots of insecurities. I know I have been guilty of looking at some of my friends and wishing I could be more like them. I see their God-given gifts and sometimes wish that I had those same gifts because they're "so much better than mine." This is one of the biggest traps Satan will set for us.

If we are too busy trying to make ourselves something we aren't, then we can't glorify God to the best of our ability. Think back on

the Olympics. What if gymnast Simone Biles really wished she could run the 400-meter dash instead? We probably wouldn't know who she is. What if rugby player Ilona Maher compared herself to Simone and only wished she could do gymnastics? She never would've put women's rugby on the map and won the US a bronze medal.

Each Olympian knows exactly what they are made for, and they own it. That's what makes them the best in the world. That's what makes them a threat. Now what if we did the exact same thing? I might not be as bubbly and welcoming as one of my friends with that gift, and I never will be. But I am good at speaking truth into people's lives. That's how God made me. So now I get to lift her up and encourage her in those gifts while stepping into the role God has for me to glorify him best.

Each of us has gifts that threaten the enemy and can be used to bring people to Christ. So don't get caught in the game of comparison and don't try to force yourself to be something you weren't made to be. What you bring to the table is exactly what God decided this world needed and is just as important as anyone else's contribution.

If we are too busy trying to make ourselves something we aren't, then we can't glorify God to the best of our ability.

Day 53

NOTHING SEPARATES YOU FROM GOD'S LOVE

ROMANS 8:38–39

Neither death nor life, nor angels nor rulers, nor things present nor things to come, nor powers, nor height nor depth, nor any other created thing will be able to separate us from the love of God that is in Christ Jesus our Lord.

My mom and I have always liked to watch old movies together. I love to see the movies she loved when she was my age, even if some of them aren't as timeless as she thinks they are. One of her favorites is *Steel Magnolias*, and I have to agree that it's a good one. Two of the characters, Truvy and Clairee, have a conversation after Truvy hires another woman, Annelle, to work at her beauty salon. Here's how it goes:

> *Truvy:* I kind of like hiring somebody with a past.
>
> *Clairee:* She can't be more than eighteen. She hasn't had time to have a past.

> *Truvy:* Oh, get with it, Clairee. This is the eighties. If you can achieve puberty, you can achieve a past.*

It's funny because it's true. If you're like me, you've already messed up and done some things that you wish you could change or take back. It's hard to be a girl growing up in this world and not struggle with so many temptations. In a weak moment, maybe you decided to get drunk with friends, maybe you went further with a boyfriend than you meant to, or maybe you said something terrible about someone. These are things that you hope your parents never find out about or that even your closest friends don't know, because you feel broken and ashamed of what you've done.

Whatever your darkest moments look like, I believe these are the very things that Satan wants us to keep hidden so that we continue to feel shame instead of God's love and forgiveness. God sees every skeleton that you've tried to shove in the back of a closet, and he still loves you more than you can even comprehend. There is no sin, no failure, no shortcoming that separates you from his love. All he wants is for you to come running back to him so he can heal the places where you've been hurt, even if that hurt was a direct result of your own dumb decisions.

Don't believe the lie that you are too messed up or too far gone. That is never true with God. And even better than that, if you allow him to, he will meet you in the very places where you feel ashamed and find a way to use even that thing for his glory. You can't outrun his plans for your life, and you can never outrun his incredible love for you.

God sees every skeleton that you've tried to shove in the back of a closet, and he still loves you more than you can even comprehend.

---

* *Steel Magnolias*, directed by Herbert Ross (TriStar Pictures, 1989), DVD, 00:14:50.

Day 54

ONLY GOD DEFINES YOU

ISAIAH 26:3–4

You will keep the mind that is dependent on you
in perfect peace,
for it is trusting in you.
Trust in the Lord forever,
because in the Lord, the Lord himself, is an everlasting rock!

I honestly don't mind conflict or confrontation that much. It's never really intimidated me, and I don't have an issue handling those problems. Something I do hate, though, is the fallout of conflict, or when friends outside of the conflict try to get involved. It is the absolute pits. That's when you have to deal with the whole "he said, she said" nonsense, and it's exhausting.

The worst part is when people slap labels on you or start rumors. You know you could prove them all wrong if you just talked to everyone, but it's out of your control and you don't have a lot of power over that. I remember when I first posted on Instagram about writing this devotional, I was so nervous about what people were going to say or think. There's a lot of anxiety that comes with worrying about other people's opinions and actions.

I remember times in high school when I would dread having to show my face around some people or felt so fed up with not having "fun" Friday night plans. It's hard to feel like maybe what people say about you is true, and even if you know it's not, it's still hard to know you have zero control over how people react or respond to you.

I can fall into a habit of self-deprecating reflection where I decide that if something goes wrong or someone doesn't like me then obviously it's all my fault. The best advice I can give on this subject is to remember that you are not defined by how others react to you. Stay close to those who lift you up and care about you, and surrender the rest of it to God. The reality is that the only thing we have control over is how we react and respond to the adversity we face.

Do we fall into the fray and try to control everything that is beyond us? Or do we remind ourselves of God's promises and what he says about us? It is said, "No weapon formed against you will succeed" (Isa. 54:17), and this includes rumors and others' actions. I know this doesn't make it easier when a guy or maybe a friend leaves you on opened on Snapchat or when others start to believe something completely untrue about you, but all you can do in those times is fix your perspective on the truth of what God says defines you. Know that you are loved and cherished and chosen for something a lot greater than what a few naysayers or critics have to say about you.

Stay close to those who lift you up and care about you, and surrender the rest of it to God.

Day 55

SWALLOWS FLOCKING

MATTHEW 10:29, 31

Aren't two sparrows sold for a penny? Yet not one of them falls to the ground without your Father's consent. . . . So don't be afraid; you are worth more than many sparrows.

One evening at sunset I was taking a walk around my neighborhood, thinking it might clear my head after a few days of restless sleep, and I went down a little path I had never seen before. It led me to a field with a little pond, and as I took in the view, I saw swallows flying in from every direction. They began to circle all around each other, swirling and diving; it almost seemed like a dance, one they performed every evening.

I watched these swallows and thought about how incredible it is that they just instinctively know this "dance." They gather in from all directions and follow God's design for their nature on instinct. All of nature does. The wolf howls to the moon, the bear tends to her cubs, and the wildflowers bloom every spring, and yet, we are worth far more than each of these creations. Isn't it funny that even though we are worth far more to Christ, we are the one creation

on this earth that doesn't follow his will or direction on instinct? It has to be our choice. We can bloom just as the wildflowers do, and we can soar to great heights just as the sparrow does, but only if we don't get in the way.

I can always tell when I'm straying from Christ because I get restless and have a hard time sleeping. It's like his gentle reminder to me that the reason for anything I am or I have is because of him. He provides his children with joy, comfort, rest, and peace, but it isn't just a one-way street. He desires a relationship with us, though he will never force it. We should ask for our heart to be close to Christ the same way the swallows roost. Daily, naturally, and instinctually.

My encouragement is that the fruit of the Spirit will be produced as long as you abide in Christ (see John 15:4). It's not always the easiest path and, yes, there will be times you will screw up, but God calls us to abide faithfully, not perfectly. I hope that provides you with some comfort.

Remember, by no means does God expect us to get things right on the first try. Can we make abiding in his will an instinct? Can we treat it the same way we need air to breathe or water to quench our thirst?

God calls us to abide faithfully, not perfectly.

THE WEEKLY RECAP

Five Truths to Remember:

1. Everyone we meet is dealing with their own problems, even if we can't see them on the surface.
2. We will never regret treating someone with kindness and compassion.
3. True, deep faith grows only when we experience God for ourselves.
4. What each person brings to the table is exactly what God decided this world needed and is just as important as anyone else's contribution.
5. We are never too far gone or messed up to be used by God.

Three Questions to Ask:

1. How can it help you to remember that everyone around you is struggling with their own issues or problems?

2. Who in your life right now can you treat with kindness and compassion, even if you don't really want to?

3. What steps can you take to deepen your relationship with God and trust him more?

Day 57

THE THING ABOUT FEAR

2 TIMOTHY 1:7

For God has not given us a spirit of fear, but one of power, love, and sound judgment.

A little fact about me that I'm not necessarily proud of is that I am terrified of bugs. I'm not talking about roly polies or butterflies but things like spiders, bees, and wasps (Oh my!). I cannot stand them. I truly hate that they exist.

I think God gave me this fear to humble me. He knew that I would be unstoppable unless I shriek every time I see something that is about .01% of my height and size. The weirdest thing though is that I'm really not bothered by a lot of things that make more sense to be afraid of. I mean, I will literally catch a snake with my bare hands and be fine, but if you put a bee near me, I'm gone. If I were to break this down logically, most snakes pose a much bigger threat to me than a bee does, but that's the funny thing about fear. It's not logical at all.

We love to stay in our comfortable bubble, and we live in a time when this strategy is promoted and encouraged. If something scares you, people will tell you things like "Well, you don't have to go through

with it" or "That's a sign you shouldn't do this." However, I'm going to say something, and I pray y'all use your own wisdom and good decision-making skills: If you want to truly become useful and if you want to step up in your faith, then guess what? You are going to have to do it scared. We are called to be bold.

As women in Christ, we need to be warriors. Do you think warriors go into battle completely unafraid of the risks? Probably not. But we have the knowledge that God has equipped us. And, yes, logically we know we are under his protection and his will, but sometimes logic doesn't prevail when we feel fear. We have to take that leap of faith while feeling a little scared, and that's completely normal. You can't just fight fear, you also have to choose to be brave. Which involves action. Do you listen to God or do you listen to the world?

We could spend our whole lives fearing so many things and never have to confront them, wasting mental energy on something Christ has already conquered. And if we do face those things, we have a God who will give us what we need to get through them. We need to remind ourselves that he is a good Father, and he is in control, no matter how big (or small, like a bee) the things we face.

If you want to step up in your faith, then guess what? You are going to have to do it scared.

Day 58

GOD SEES THINGS WE DON'T

PROVERBS 3:5–7

Listen for God's voice in everything you do, everywhere you go;
he's the one who will keep you on track.
Don't assume that you know it all.
Run to God! Run from evil! (MSG)

Sometimes it can be really hard to understand what God is doing. We go through hard situations, we see tragedy, or we watch loved ones struggle, and our first thought is usually, *Why God?* We want to comprehend what's happening. I mean, how much easier would it be if we could see the bigger picture or even get a glimpse a few years down the road and be like, *Oh yeah, I can handle this because of x, y, z later on.* Unfortunately, that's not how life works, and that's not how our God works.

We have to remind ourselves that we serve a holy, all-knowing, and all-powerful God, and we are only human. Our comprehension and logic have so many limits while our God is limitless and has infinite wisdom. I

mean, people dedicate their whole lives to theology and understanding God, yet they barely scratch the surface. I even have friends who aren't believers, who say their lack of belief is because, logically, it just doesn't make sense, and my only response is, "Well, you're absolutely right. It doesn't make sense." In my opinion the biggest solution to all of this is humility. We want to control or fix the hard times instead of embracing and surrendering them to God. We won't always be able to grasp the knowledge of his ways while we are in the middle of a struggle or when our plans don't turn out the way we hoped.

What if we just take a deep breath and say, "I'm not in control, but I trust the one who is"?

In life, there will always be situations outside our control. And that's the point. God wants us to trust him to provide and to protect, and it's no wonder we get so freaked out—we were never meant to handle it all alone. We were never meant to lean on our own understanding or logic. Instead, we can remember these truths: God is good, God is ever-present, God is sovereign, and God is full of grace and mercy and love for us.

That doesn't mean everything is going to feel better. You will still hurt, you will still struggle, and—speaking from experience—you will still be frustrated a lot of the time. But the good news is those feelings and struggles are not the truth or reality of the situation. The truth is that God has already walked the road before you and will help you fight the giants along the way to end up on the path he paved for you.

God is good. God is ever-present. God is sovereign, and God is full of grace and mercy and love for us.

Day 59

ON BEING SWEET

PROVERBS 16:24

Gracious words are a honeycomb,
sweet to the soul and healing to the bones. (NIV)

Here's the thing about me: I'm rarely called "sweet." It's kind of funny considering that my mom literally chose my name because of the song "Sweet Caroline" by Neil Diamond and even she will say that I'm usually a little more salty than sweet. But what I've learned as I've grown older is that there is a difference between being sweet and being kind. I always do my best to be kind to those around me. Sweetness is often more about wanting people to like you because you're nice instead of kindness, which can be more like respecting those around you enough to speak the truth in love.

But I have learned that it's important to speak kind words over the people God puts in your life. We never know what someone else is going through, what hard time they are currently in the middle of, or how God might use us to speak words of encouragement and wisdom when they are most needed.

The other day I was walking across campus when a woman I'd never met before looked at me and said, "Well, you're the cutest thing I've seen today." It was such a small comment, but it brought a little bit of joy and happiness to my day—just one simple moment of feeling seen by someone. There have been days at work when my boss has taken the time to compliment me on doing my job well, and it has never failed to make me feel good.

Those happy moments are a reminder to me to find opportunities to tell people when I see something of value in who they are or what they are doing. How different would our schools, our communities, and our world look if we all took the time to remember what it might mean if we spoke life and truth over the people around us? There are always going to be people who choose to focus on the negative, but God has given us eyes to see the good in those around us and mouths to speak words that could heal them where they have been hurt. There is so much more power in healing what is broken as opposed to poking at old wounds that might already be battered and bruised. I want to encourage you (and remind myself) to build up the people God has placed in your life.

There are always going to be people who choose to focus on the negative, but God has given us eyes to see the good in those around us.

Day 60

HEALING WHAT IS BROKEN

JEREMIAH 33:6

Yet I will certainly bring health and healing to it and will indeed heal them. I will let them experience the abundance of true peace.

As an athlete, I have seen my fair share of injuries on the playing field. One of the worst I ever saw happened during my senior season. We were in the middle of a game when my teammate's leg collided directly with another girl's leg as they were fighting for the ball. You could hear the crack like a gunshot throughout the stadium. It echoed loudly as the crowd grew silent. After an examination, the trainers determined that she had broken her shin. So much for those shin guards they insist we wear.

The injury was brutal—and fixing it was terrible as well. It seemed so counterintuitive. Because her shin was only partially broken, they couldn't just set it. Instead, the surgeons had to fully break the bone in order to make sure it would heal properly. Not a fun process.

I can look back at the times when people have really hurt me, whether it was a bad breakup or girls being straight-up cruel, and when I pray for healing from those times, God makes me process and

walk through those old wounds. We have to face the pain, the ugly, and those feelings of anger and sadness. If we try to avoid them, they can become just like an improperly set bone that leaves you crippled.

It is not weak to mourn a loss or the past. That's actually the strongest, healthiest thing you can do. There is a time to process the hurt, but then it is time to surrender it to God as well. And just like physical injuries, you can't necessarily see the healing as it's taking place. You just have to trust the process. Every day, things will start feeling a little better. Moving forward will become a little easier until a day comes when you realize you're moving like normal. Emotional injuries are the same way. Every day you have to choose to believe that God is working on putting you back together. You might not get the closure you want or the apology you deserve, but you can trust that God will heal you and take care of the situation. He will always restore the places where your heart has been broken.

There is a time to process the hurt, but then it is time to surrender it to God as well.

Day 61

THE BATTLE IN OUR MIND

GALATIANS 5:17

For the flesh desires what is against the Spirit, and the Spirit desires what is against the flesh; these are opposed to each other, so that you don't do what you want.

There have been seasons in my life when I have rolled out of bed in the morning both ticked off *and* filled with dread. The idea of going through my day was just discouraging and I didn't feel like I had the strength to deal with all the nonsense I might face. Some of you may relate to this feeling, whether it's not wanting to face the reality of spending another weekend with your parents instead of a fun friend group, a bad breakup where you know you're going to have to see your ex at school, or the aftermath of doing something embarrassing at a party. Facing the consequences in the morning light seems dreadful.

I wish there was something I could tell you that would completely ease that feeling, but unfortunately that's not really how our minds work. What I have learned is that sometimes it's mind over matter. It's focusing on what is actually true instead of the spiral of lies that can

take over your brain. For me, I make the decision that I will not allow Satan's lies to stop me from living life and fighting for joy every day.

The tricky thing about our feelings is that they are from the flesh, and the flesh is always fighting our spirit. Every day is a battle for our mind, whether we want it to be or not. We have to speak the truth of God over ourselves every day and remember where our identity is found, even if our heart tries to tell us something different.

For example, David may have been scared when he faced Goliath. I'm sure there were whispers in his mind trying to tell him he was just a young shepherd boy, but he stood on the fact that God had delivered him before and would deliver him again. His identity was in something so much greater than his reality, and that is the mentality we need to have when we wake up in the morning.

In the moments when we are filled with anxiety, doubt, or dread, we need to remember there is so much more to our lives than our circumstances or failures. Even as we anticipate a rough day ahead, we can remember that our God has already conquered the day and walked it before us. That doesn't mean it's going to feel easy, but it means we were delivered before the day even started.

So whatever you might be nervous to face today or this week or this month, face it with your head held high, knowing there are great things in store for you, and God is going before you, providing what you need to persevere one day at a time.

There is so much more to our lives than our circumstances or failures.

Day 62

WHAT A FRIEND LOOKS LIKE

PROVERBS 18:24

Friends come and friends go,
but a true friend sticks by you like family. (MSG)

I think sometimes, either because of social media or movies or maybe some other reason, we love to romanticize friendships. We desire to have the giant friend group that gets along or these close friends who are more like sisters to us. We envision growing old together and always being close.

And while this can be great when everyone involved is emotionally healthy, it's important to make sure we are not placing this ideal over whatever our reality might be.

Sure, on social media the posts featuring a giant friend group that is beautifully filtered and drama-free looks good, but what is the reality? Is it really emotionally healthy or is this group gossiping behind each other's backs and filled with infighting? Something I have seen in a lot of female friendships is girls who compromise or put up with

being mistreated because the relationship still "looks" like what they want. Girls will tolerate other girls tearing them down if it means they can stay in the friend group because they are more scared of being alone. Instead, we need to know our worth and live from that truth.

Maybe you even have a friend that has some really good days and everything seems great, then she'll just exclude you one night or go hang out with girls who were so mean to you. Here's what I'm going to tell you: That's not a real friend; that's a counterfeit.

True friends build you up; they rally behind you and stand by your side. They push you closer to God and want you to be the best you can be. They are not going to be perfect, but their hearts will be in the right place. They aren't going to have ulterior motives, and you won't feel nervous and worry that they're going to talk about you behind your back when you leave the room. I have been in seasons when I had to make the decision to either compromise with the counterfeit or set boundaries and put my faith in the fact that God is going to bring the right people into my life in his timing. Setting boundaries can be hard and it can hurt, even if you know it's the right thing. But remember your worth and know that you deserve better than someone who throws backhanded compliments your way like candy. You deserve friends who champion you and love you like family, and even if they're not in your life right now, trust in God's timing and know that they will be.

You deserve friends who champion you and love you like family.

THE WEEKLY RECAP

Five Truths to Remember:

1. If we're going to truly grow in our faith, we have to be bold and make the hard decisions even when we feel scared.
2. God sees things in our life and in our future that we don't.
3. There are always going to be people who choose to focus on the negative, but God can give us eyes to see the good in those around us and the mouth to speak words that might have the power to heal them where they have been hurt.
4. We might not get the closure we want or the apology we deserve, but we can trust that God will heal us and take care of the situation.
5. There is so much more to life than our current circumstances or failures.

Three Questions to Ask:

1. What leap of faith is God asking you to take even though you feel scared?

2. Where can you choose to focus on the positive and speak words of healing and truth to someone in your life?

3. Where are you holding on to unforgiveness from the past because you didn't get closure or an apology? Can you trust God enough to let go?

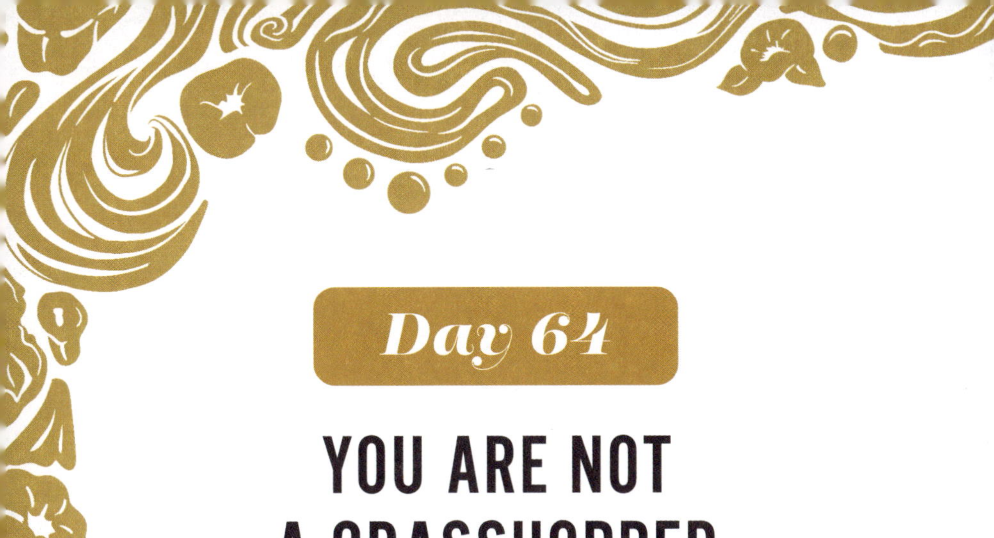

Day 64

YOU ARE NOT A GRASSHOPPER

NUMBERS 13:33

To ourselves we seemed like grasshoppers, and we must have seemed the same to them.

There have been times in my life when I've had to face a fear that seemed almost impossible to conquer. The kind of moment where I would've rather stayed in bed than deal with whatever was going on. Moments like when I had to walk into school and felt like I had no friends left—it was unknown and intimidating to walk in those school hallways—or when my parents dropped me off at college. While I was excited about starting a new chapter, I also felt a little lonely and scared about the future. I felt small and maybe a little vulnerable, like a grasshopper, in these situations.

In Numbers 13, the children of Israel are on the verge of walking into the land God promised them. Twelve men go investigate the land but only two men, Joshua and Caleb, come back believing the Israelites can conquer what lies ahead. The other ten see

only the obstacles and all the reasons simply walking into the promised land won't work. They had lost sight of the faithfulness of God and let their fear take over. It is their land, but they have to be brave enough to take it. To take hold of the new, we have to face our fears and let go of the old and the familiar.

I know how hard this can be. We love what feels familiar because it's comfortable and it's known. Leaving behind what we know for something we can't fully see yet is scary. But are we going to make the foundation of our life faith or fear? What we choose will determine how we make decisions and if we will allow God to make our lives all that he wants them to be.

We can look at a situation and think it is impossible. We see how big the obstacles are and how hard it might be to overcome them, but we discount that God is with us. If it is part of his plan for our life, then he will help us take hold of what he has for us. Our trials and our fears are opportunities to trust in a God who sees all things and has promised he's working all things for our good. At times, he's going to call us to walk into a new land, a new adventure, a new season—and he has good for you there. The future is your promised land. He already knows your whole story. The beginning. The end. The giants you will face. And everything in between.

Remember, you are not a grasshopper; you are a child of God. Don't be afraid to walk into a new land, knowing that he is there waiting for you.

To take hold of the new, we have to face our fears and let go of the old and the familiar.

Day 65

TRUST WHAT GOD IS BUILDING

ISAIAH 54:11

Afflicted city, lashed by storms and not comforted,
I will rebuild you with stones of turquoise,
your foundations with lapis lazuli. (NIV)

It can be hard to stand on your own sometimes. God designed us for relationships and community, so when we are in a season lacking those things, it can really be a challenge. You open up Instagram and see these precious couples supporting and loving each other, or a really close friend group figuring out life together, and it feels lonely. You see people leaning on each other and it reminds you that maybe you don't have that in this season or, at least, not in the way you hoped.

As I write this, I'm feeling a little bit of grief and maybe envy as I see my friends getting engaged or falling in love with a guy who's supporting them. I'm happy for them, and their happiness doesn't mean I won't eventually find my own, but it still stings a little. But

even if my community looks different than I thought it would at this point in life, that doesn't make this season any less of a blessing. Our situations are exactly what we make of them, and having the right perspective is so important.

God loves you dearly and while he may not come down from heaven to give you a hug, he is no less present in your life. His hand is moving and working on what is seen and unseen. While it seems like a cliché to tell you to focus on Jesus, it really is the only thing that will build you up when you feel a little lonely.

You are in this season for a purpose. It's easy to focus on what we don't have, but we can choose to use this time to focus instead on what God has for us and how he is working to make us better, stronger, and more connected to him.

Sometimes when God has plans for us, he removes anything that could take our focus away from him. This truth has pushed me and grown me more than I think I even realize, but everything he is building in me is for a purpose much greater than myself. So, if you find yourself in a season that feels lonely, find your strength in God, talk it out with him, and ask him for wisdom on how you can grow during this time.

God loves you dearly and while he may not come down from heaven to give you a hug, he is no less present in your life.

Day 66

THE DIFFERENCE GRATITUDE CAN MAKE

1 SAMUEL 12:24

Above all, fear the Lord and worship him faithfully with all your heart; consider the great things he has done for you.

There are days when I wake up and feel completely overwhelmed. Maybe I haven't studied for the test I have to take that afternoon the way I should have. Or maybe I'm caught up in feeling anxious about my future. I'm about to go into my senior year of college and don't necessarily feel equipped or prepared to be an actual grown-up with a job and responsibilities. The fear of the unknown can spiral into me trying to figure out what the next five years of my life will look like and the next thing I know, I'm worried about turning thirty even though I just turned twenty-one.

These types of worries are not helpful for anyone.

You may relate. Maybe you're in a season where your group of friends seems a little shaky and you feel lonely. Or things at home are just difficult as you try to get your family to respect that you are growing up and want more freedom. There could be a hard diagnosis or maybe your parents are going through a divorce. Maybe you're in the middle of college applications and have no idea where you will even be in the next year or so. These seasons hold so much weight, and they can feel intimidating.

Here's something I've learned as I've looked for ways to deal with my fear and anxiety: Gratitude is a strong way to reduce anxiety. The two things—gratitude and anxiety—actually cannot coexist in the brain. In fact, gratitude has the ability to strengthen relationships, improve mental health, and minimize stress.* These all seem like good things.

When you feel anxious about the future, train yourself to take a deep breath and think of what you're grateful for right this moment. This can be as simple as, *Well, I woke up today. There's still air in my lungs so God must want to use me.* When you take a moment to inventory what you are grateful for, you begin to realize that even though life isn't perfect, God has given you so many good things. Do you have a family who loves you? Do you have friends who will listen to you? Do you have the option to attend college or pursue a career that you're excited about? Did you drink an exceptionally good Dr Pepper today? Don't overlook how important it is to walk through life with gratitude and find the positive moments where you can. God has given you these gifts to help point your heart back to him, so trust him for what is ahead, knowing he has been faithful so far.

When you feel anxious about the future, train yourself to take a deep breath and think of what you're grateful for right this moment.

---

* Geyze Diniz et al., "The Effects of Gratitude Interventions: A Systematic Review and Meta-Analysis," *National Library of Medicine* 21 (August 2023), https://www.ncbi.nlm.nih.gov/pmc/articles/PMC10393216/.

Day 67

WHEN THE UNEXPECTED SHOWS UP

JAMES 1:2–3

Consider it a great joy, my brothers and sisters, whenever you experience various trials, because you know that the testing of your faith produces endurance.

When I was in high school, I worked at the local vet clinic, which led to some pretty interesting experiences. One day we had to examine and vaccinate a cat named Bob. When I walked in, all I could see was a ball of brown fur flying around the room and yowling so loud that I thought my eardrums might bleed. Then a glass jar shattered, and the doctor yelled, "GET THE NET!" It was at that moment when I realized we had severely underestimated Bob. But in our defense, we went in thinking, *How bad can a cat named Bob actually be?*

You could say Bob is a metaphor for my high school experience. Just as the vet tech and I expected Bob to be sweet, people raved about how high school would be the best years of my life. (Spoiler alert: They were wrong.) What I learned is that high school isn't

meant to be when you peak, but it is crucial to figuring out who you want to become. It will help you develop the strength and character you will need as you move into your future. It helps you develop a foundation in your faith, and the trials you go through during this time will prepare you for so much more later on.

During those years, I found myself identifying with Chris Traeger from *Parks and Recreation* when he said, "If I keep my body moving, and my mind occupied at all times, I will avoid falling into a bottomless pit of despair."*

High school didn't look like I had planned, so I had to choose: Was I going to let it break me or make me stronger? I've always believed that good things come from adversity, but this was the first time that belief had been put to the test.

Ultimately, I decided it was time to stop trying to be comfortable and start embracing change. I moved on from a group of friends who weren't good for me, I broke up with a boyfriend who wasn't right, and I focused on ways I could learn from what I'd been through. I learned life is better when you are running your best race and leaving your failures and disappointments behind. The fact is life is sometimes a lot like an angry, unpredictable cat named Bob who shows up and trashes the place.

God uses every bit of those unexpected things to give you grit and resilience. Trust him even when the feral cats show up, knowing that God will often use the unexpected or hard moments to lead to something better than you ever imagined.

Life is better when you are running your best race and leaving your failures and disappointments behind.

---

* *Parks and Recreation*, season 4, episode 21, "Bus Tour," directed by Dean Holland, written by Aisha Muharrar and Alan Yang, aired May 3, 2012, on NBC.

Day 68

DEVELOPING WHAT WILL LAST

MATTHEW 7:24

Therefore, everyone who hears these words of mine and acts on them will be like a wise man who built his house on the rock.

Growing up, I spent a lot of free moments practicing soccer. Even though I kind of hated it at the time, some of my favorite memories are of my dad taking me through speed, strength, and conditioning drills. He made me practice after I was exhausted, when I thought I had nothing left.

The point he always exaggerated was that I couldn't just know what I was doing, it had to become muscle memory. I had to know how to shoot, dribble, pass, and make a move without second-guessing myself. He told me that when it comes down to a moment that counts, your knowledge is not going to be leading you but your instinct and muscle memory will. He wanted to make sure that when I had nothing left, I could fall back on all of my training, because those instincts would allow me to handle the situation and not make it worse.

The only way to achieve true muscle memory is through practice, practice, practice, repetition, repetition, repetition. That same logic can be used for anything in life but especially with our faith. It takes practice and repetition to develop faith, and you develop it one step at a time through discipline and focusing on what is important. Faith grows when you feel like you have nothing left to give, almost like a muscle.

Think of it like a foundation for a house. We have to depend on the foundation of our faith to keep us steady when the rain comes or when the storms hit. Please notice how I say *when* and not *if*.

Because the truth is storms will come and trials are going to occur in your life. The time to build a strong foundation is not during the storm but before it comes rolling in. Just like how my dad pushed me to have strength and speed before I ever needed those skills for a game, the time to learn is not when something happens but before it does so we have instincts to fall back on.

In life we have to prepare for the moments that count because we never know when they will come. Just like David with the lion and the bear, God fills our lives with little moments that shape, build, and prepare our foundation. Though something may seem small or unimportant at the time, don't discredit the way it is training your spirit and mind for bigger battles later on.

The time to build a strong foundation is not during the storm but before it comes rolling in.

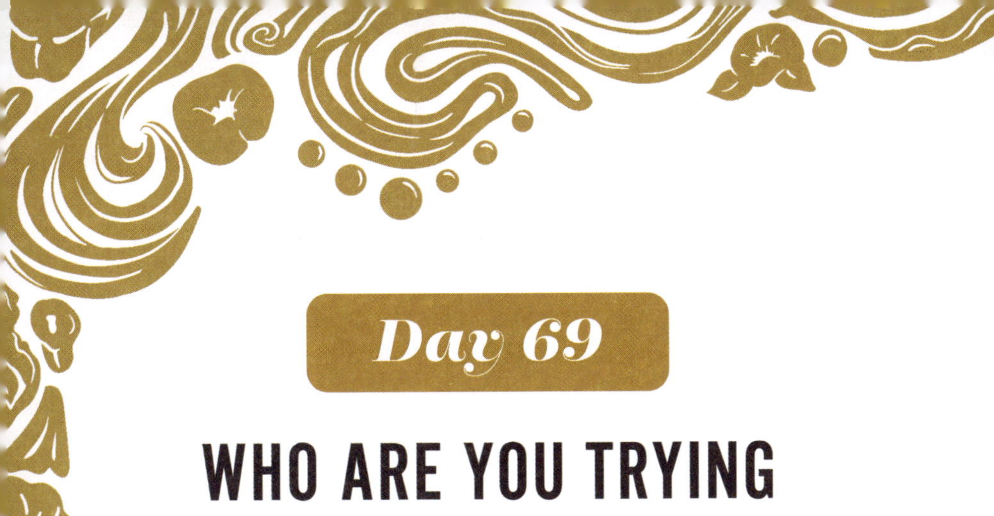

Day 69

WHO ARE YOU TRYING TO PLEASE?

GALATIANS 1:10

For am I now trying to persuade people, or God? Or am I striving to please people? If I were still trying to please people, I would not be a servant of Christ.

You are not going to be liked by everyone you meet. And you are not going to like everyone you meet either. That's completely normal. We all have different personalities, and some of those personalities are going to clash.

But this becomes an issue when we try to change ourselves to be more likable. An interesting truth I once heard someone share is that pleasing people is a form of manipulation. Even if it's under the guise of being kind, you aren't living the truth because you are diminishing yourself to appease someone else. Jesus literally lived the perfect life and he was still hated. If the most perfect man was hated, none of us really have a chance.

There have been moments when I tried so hard to fit myself in a box because I really wanted to make something work. I tried to be different than how God designed me because I sought the approval of people more than God. Full transparency, this only led to lots of anxiety and heartbreak. No relationship, job, or future is worth sacrificing who God created you to be. He has something planned for you that will be real and not a counterfeit version.

It can be scary to be fully yourself in this world because rejection hurts. What if people don't like what they see when what they see is the real you? There is a vulnerability that comes with being unapologetically yourself, and no one really wants to talk about that. I believe this fear comes from the false belief that we can control how people perceive us. We think if we act or look a certain way, we can stop someone from walking away or avoid rejection, but we can't.

At some point, if someone isn't meant to be in your life, they are going to leave, no matter what. God has walked this road ahead of you. He knows all the people who are going to cherish and love you exactly as you are. He also knows those who you might not get along with. Most importantly, he knows the lives you are going to change with your specific, wonderful personality. He sees all and he sees the people that you are going to bring closer to him because of your talkative personality, your blunt humor, or your overly competitive nature. Trust that he has great plans for you exactly as you are and find your identity in that, not in the opinions of others.

No relationship, job, or future is worth sacrificing who God created you to be.

THE WEEKLY RECAP

Five Truths to Remember:

1. To take hold of the new, we have to face our fears and let go of the old and the familiar.
2. There is purpose in every season of life.
3. Gratitude helps diminish anxiety.
4. Life is better when we quit focusing on our failures and disappointments.
5. No relationship, job, or future is worth sacrificing who God created us to be.

Three Questions to Ask:

1. Is there something you are holding on to because it's familiar but God is asking you to let it go?

2. What are five things you have to be grateful for in your life right now?

3. Look at the season you are currently in or a season you have been in. How has God used that season in your life?

Day 71

WHEN IT'S TIME TO WALK AWAY

DEUTERONOMY 1:6

The LORD our God spoke to us at Horeb: "You have stayed at this mountain long enough."

It's hard to know when you should fight for something and when God is telling you it's time to let that person or situation go.

This is where the children of Israel found themselves after years of wandering around the desert on the way to the promised land. They had camped at the bottom of Mount Horeb for almost a year. They used that time to be restored and to reflect on all they had been through before they took the next step of entering into the land God had for them. I'm guessing that they had grown comfortable there because, even though the land might have been barren, it was at least familiar and less scary than entering something unknown and uncertain.

It's so hard for all of us to walk away from people or places that feel comfortable. Maybe you're in the middle of trying to figure out

if it's time to end a relationship or to pivot and follow a new dream. I have been in this exact situation so many times. It's hard to leave behind what is familiar when we don't know what's coming next.

God takes us places that we're meant to stay for only a season. They are a part of our journey but were never intended to be the final destination. It's just a place he uses in our life to help us grow and change and, hopefully, learn to trust him more. And like the Israelites camped at Mount Horeb, when the purpose of that place has been achieved, he tells us it's time to move on.

We can choose to stay, but then we will miss out on all God has ahead for us. He will never ask you to move on from something if he doesn't have something better waiting up ahead. We may not always be able to see it clearly at the time, and it may feel really scary, but trusting him enough to walk away from places that he no longer wants us in will help our faith grow stronger and will teach us to trust him more. He sees your value so much more clearly than you do and doesn't want you to settle for anything less than all the good things he has in store for you.

God takes us places that we're meant to stay for only a season.

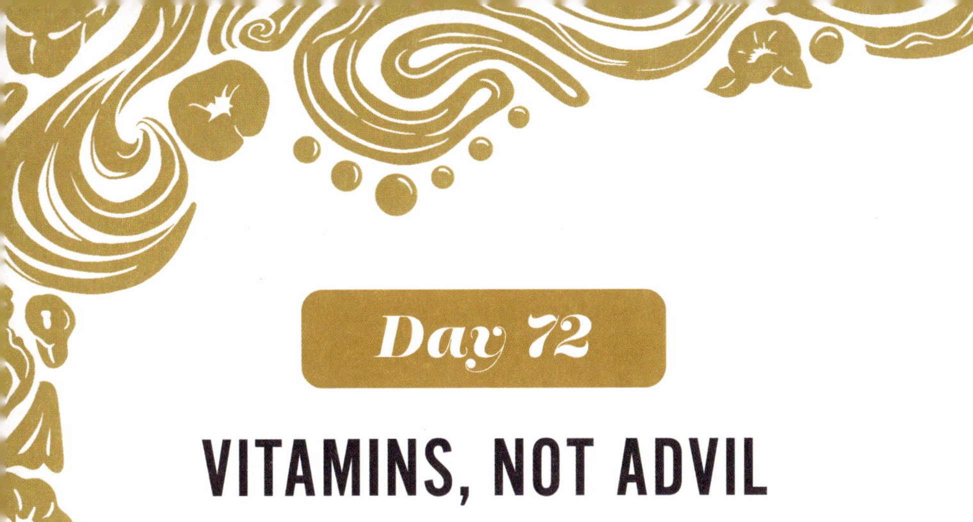

Day 72

VITAMINS, NOT ADVIL

JOHN 4:14

But whoever drinks from the water that I will give him will never get thirsty again. In fact, the water I will give him will become a well of water springing up in him for eternal life.

I know there have been times when I have opened the Bible looking for a quick fix. I've wondered, *How can this Scripture make me feel better? How can I feel closer to God? How can reading this fix my mistakes?* Why do we do this? Going into a friendship with purely selfish intentions is looked down on, but we can slip into the habit of thinking it's okay with God.

The reality is God wants a relationship with us, and a healthy relationship goes both ways. Who wants that friend who calls only when bad things are happening in their life? We need to attempt to know him the way he knows us (even though it's impossible).

One way to build a strong relationship is to take the time to open our Bible. This practice will help you learn more about him: what he loves, what he hates, and how he handles situations. It will help you know which way he wants you to go in life and will give you hope and

trust in your future. You can come to him with your struggles, your dreams, your disappointments, your questions, and your heartbreaks. He wants to hear all of it.

Though Scripture can sometimes make us feel better, that's not necessarily the main intention of reading it. A friend of mine once said, "Placing Scripture over something makes it holy, not feel better." We want to treat Scripture like Advil—using it to soothe an ache or to fix an issue—but Scripture should be treated a lot more like a vitamin. It's something you take daily, even when you feel fine, to maintain and protect your health. It is supposed to sustain and nourish, not just fix or soothe.

Reading the Bible daily can be hard. I know there are a lot of days when I am definitely not in the mood or feel too tired or busy to sit down and take the time to learn more about God, but I think that's where a perspective shift needs to happen. Everything else in our lives is static noise compared to our spiritual well-being. If our spiritual health isn't in tune, then everything else will soon be off as well.

I want to encourage you to seek a relationship with God, not just a religion where you check the boxes to be a "good Christian." God desperately wants to know you and for you to know him. Think about someone you love hanging out with, and then think about the idea of them canceling on you. It would hurt your feelings. Don't you think it's the same for God when it comes to us?

Scripture is supposed to sustain and nourish, not just fix or soothe.

Day 73

FOR SUCH A TIME AS THIS

ESTHER 4:14

If you keep silent at this time, relief and deliverance will come to the Jewish people from another place, but you and your father's family will be destroyed.

The story of Queen Esther is one of my favorites in the Bible. I love hearing how God used strong women for his purposes and plans, especially in a time when women weren't always valued in society. Plus, there are so many layers to Esther's testimony. I love a complex queen.

When I first read the book of Esther, I thought it seemed like a story about a beautiful girl who goes to the palace, gets some beauty treatments, ends up being the queen, and saves her people from being killed. You know, just your basic Tuesday. But the reality is things in life hadn't really gone Esther's way. She was orphaned at a young age, then was taken away from her home and her people and found herself in a foreign palace, which was a place she didn't necessarily want to be. I mean, I love a spa day but how many facials make up for being forced to marry a king who may decide to have you killed?

When her cousin Mordecai sent word that her people were in danger of being killed, Esther could have chosen to stay silent and do nothing. But I believe that Esther and Mordecai both knew God had put her in this position for a reason, so Esther made a plan. She prayed, she asked the people around her to pray, and then she had the wisdom and the courage to act on what God was calling her to do. She chose to be brave. She knew the only voice that mattered in her life was the voice of God.

We don't have to stay stuck in fear when difficult situations come into our lives. Even if you feel like you're "just a girl," God will give you the strength to face what he is calling you to do.

Sometimes the places we find ourselves or the people God puts in our life aren't really about us but about what he wants to do through us. He always has a bigger plan than what we see on the surface.

God will help you know when to keep quiet and wait and when to speak out. He never leaves us in difficult situations. The secret to Esther being used "for such a time as this" wasn't because of her beauty or her position but her faith in an unshakable God. We have that same power in our lives, even if we don't have all the free beauty treatments.

God will give you the strength to face what he is calling you to do.

Day 74

THE HIGH ROAD, NOT THE EASY ROAD

2 TIMOTHY 2:23–25

Refuse to get involved in inane discussions; they always end up in fights. God's servant must not be argumentative, but a gentle listener and a teacher who keeps cool, working firmly but patiently with those who refuse to obey. (MSG)

When I was in tenth grade, a guy at my school was threatened by me because he knew I always stood for what I believed in and wasn't intimidated by him. He came to me one day and said if I didn't start spreading rumors about a certain girl, he was going to make sure rumors got spread around about me.

I had a decision to make. I could compromise my morals to save my own skin or I could say no, which would mean losing people I thought were close to me. A part of me really wanted to take the easy route, be comfortable, and save myself. But then I realized something: I had God. This gave me hope in something far greater than my circumstances. No matter what happened, I would get through

this because my God was going to take care of me and give me the strength I needed. The other girl didn't have that. She was alone and vulnerable, and sadly, her faith was only in the people around her. She wouldn't be able to withstand the storm that was coming but I could.

So I told that guy I would never betray another person like that. It sucked. I lost my friends, and people were so mean to me. Even worse, the girl I was trying to help spread rumors about me and harassed me. It was so hard to understand why this was happening when I had done my best to do what I knew was right.

This isn't a feel-good story to start your day, but I'm sharing it because you may have been through something similar or are currently dealing with rumors, lies, or betrayal from people you thought were your friends. There will be so many times in life that a situation won't seem fair, but God will give you the strength to walk through it without sinking to the level of people around you who aren't following him. Resist the urge to play the same stupid games as the people around you, whether it's out of their own insecurities or just a mean heart. Trust that God will bring real, true friends into your life and that he will always be with you no matter what you face.

God will always be with you no matter what you face.

Day 75

NEVER-ENDING MERCY AND GRACE

LAMENTATIONS 3:22–24

Because of the Lord's faithful love
we do not perish,
for his mercies never end.
They are new every morning;
great is your faithfulness!
I say, "The Lord is my portion,
therefore I will put my hope in him."

It is inevitable that we are going to mess up. We are going to fall short, we will stray from God, we'll doubt, and we'll fear. We are going to struggle with falling back into sin no matter how hard we try and despite all our best efforts.

The beauty of the gospel though is that our sins are forgiven and that our identity is never in our failure because we have a loving and merciful God. I know we all know this and have heard this truth since first becoming a believer, but do we really understand it? We may

have a hard time really comprehending God's mercy because it's so much bigger than our human mindset can fathom.

We might even believe that this grace can definitely be true for others, while struggling to extend that same mercy and love to ourselves. I really know my heart and all of my ugliness personally. I see my selfishness and failures, and I know that I am definitely not as good as I should be. It makes it hard to understand that even though God knows everything about me and sees all my flaws and failures, he still wants me to be his. I don't believe that I'm the only one who feels this way though. We just don't like to talk about it or say it out loud to others.

It's a lie the enemy loves to throw at us. He wants us to feel alone in our failures and our struggles. But let this be your reminder today: You are not alone, and every other Christian has felt the same way that you may feel right now.

It's easy to believe the lie that after a certain number of failures, God's mercy will start to run out. We might believe that he'll forgive us once or twice for that one sin, but what about the tenth, eleventh, or five hundredth time?

The truth is God's mercies never end. He does not say things he doesn't mean. The thought that God is going to run out of patience with us is a straight-up lie from Satan whose goal is to make us feel distant from God, when in reality, God wants us to run back to him as soon as we can. He is always waiting, ready to forgive again. No matter what you've done, even for the tenth time this week, you can never exhaust God's forgiveness and love for you.

The beauty of the gospel though is that our sins are forgiven and that our identity is never in our failure.

Day 76

WHAT LOYALTY LOOKS LIKE

RUTH 1:16

For wherever you go, I will go,
and wherever you live, I will live;
your people will be my people,
and your God will be my God.

I love the story of Ruth. Most of the focus of this story is on Ruth meeting Boaz, but none of that would have happened if not for Ruth's stubbornness and loyalty to her mother-in-law, Naomi.

When the story begins, both women are experiencing grief. Ruth's husband has just died and Naomi has lost both her sons and her husband. It looks like Ruth's best, safest option is to go back to Moab where she is from, and Naomi encourages her to do exactly that. But instead, Ruth makes a decision based on loyalty and love and tells Naomi, "For wherever you go, I will go," making it clear she has no plans to leave her.

Ruth ends up providing for them by gleaning in the fields and, ultimately, this leads to her meeting Boaz. I love this fierce, unselfish loyalty from Ruth even though she didn't know how much it may cost her.

It makes me think of the friends in my life who have been loyal to me through hard times. The ones who stood up for me when people around me were saying things about me that weren't true. The ones who showed up during a bad breakup and made sure I had ice cream and someone to watch dumb movies with. The ones I can call at any time and know they will show up. The ones who won't talk about me behind my back. Those are the types of friends who make me feel safe and loved because I know my heart is safe in their hands.

These people aren't always easy to find, but I've learned that one of the ways to find that kind of friend is to be that kind of friend. There are so many voices that will tell you to look out for yourself or to do what feels best to you, but there is so much more value in standing by a friend going through a hard time or being there to listen even when it's not easy. Real friendship sometimes looks like sacrificing what you want for what is good for someone else. This is how you build true relationships and it's how you find the people who will stay by your side no matter what comes.

Real friendship sometimes looks like sacrificing what you want for what is good for someone else.

Day 77

THE WEEKLY RECAP

Five Truths to Remember:

1. There are places and people that God puts in our lives only for a season.
2. Spending time reading the Bible is important for our spiritual health.
3. God will give us the strength to do anything he asks us to do.
4. God will bring real, true friends into our lives.
5. Real friendship sometimes looks like sacrificing what we want for what is good for someone else.

Three Questions to Ask:

1. Can you think of friends or situations that God brought into your life for only a season? What was the purpose of those people and moments and how did God use them in your life?

2. How can you spend more time reading the Bible, keeping in mind that this is a huge way that God speaks to you?

3. What are the areas in your life where you need God to give you strength right now?

Day 78

HOLDING PLANS LOOSELY

PROVERBS 19:21

Many are the plans in a person's heart,
but it is the Lord's purpose that prevails. (NIV)

I hate to tell you this, but sometimes we make plans in our head that won't turn out like we thought they would. Thank you for reading. You're welcome for the encouragement. Have a great day.

But, seriously, it's the truth. When I started high school, I thought I wanted to play soccer in college. Then I had two bad injuries that changed that dream for me. I started college and thought I wanted to become a veterinarian. Then I took biology and chemistry at the same time and realized this was not the life I wanted. I've had friendships that didn't work out the way I hoped, and I've dated someone that I thought might be the one only to have it not work out. And every time my plans or dreams have been detoured, I've had to trust that God knows what he is doing because he sees the whole picture of what is going to be best for me and what will ultimately bring me joy.

This can be applied in so many different ways in your life. So much is going to change and that's okay. I want to encourage you to roll

with it and keep an open mind. My friend groups have changed, my major has changed, my plans for my career have changed. So many things ebb and flow in our lives. I have been nervous every single time something has changed but, ultimately, that change has always been what's best for me. God has your back. Everything you go through and every dream that doesn't turn out like you thought it would is on purpose, not because he forgot your plan.

These years of your life are going to bring so much change, and not all of it is going to look the way you hoped or envisioned. Failure is inevitable. Doors are going to close on you, and that's completely okay because twice as many are going to open, and they will be the right doors.

It's so normal to dream about the future and to have hopes and plans for what it might bring, but remember, God's wisdom is deeper than ours and we need to hold our plans with an open hand. It can be so heartbreaking to surrender what we thought we wanted, but keep in mind that God is always working everything for our good in ways that we cannot always clearly see.

God's wisdom is deeper than ours and we need to hold our plans with an open hand.

Day 79

PURSUING PEACE

1 PETER 3:11–12

And let him turn away from evil
and do what is good.
Let him seek peace and pursue it,
because the eyes of the Lord are on the righteous
and his ears are open to their prayer.

There is no way to go through life without conflict. People are going to let you down and betray your trust. Or maybe you're the one to blame. You hurt someone, even if that wasn't your intent. When I was going through a lot of struggles with my group of friends during high school, all I wanted to do was find a way to talk it out so we could make things better and get back to the way we used to be. Sometimes that's a realistic possibility and sometimes there's just no real way to mend what has been broken. Either way, God calls us to pursue peace with everyone around us, but peace can look different in the different situations we face.

And this can be hard because sometimes instead of pursuing peace, what we really want to do is burn it all down. We feel let down, betrayed, and angry. This is how we know we need Jesus. Peace is great when it comes easy, but it can be quite a challenge when we have to work for it. It can be especially hard when you find yourself in the middle of drama about who said what about who and who did what terrible thing last weekend and which friend lied about something you said to another friend. Raise your hand if you've been there, and please see me raising my hand with you.

The key is to first ask God to give you the peace you need by remembering that he is in control of this situation. We can't control what others may say or do to us, but we can remember that God is always with us, even in the middle of a hurtful situation. Then you must ask yourself if you trust him enough to believe that he will give you the grace you need to pursue peace with the people who have hurt you or who you have hurt.

There will be times when forgiving and reconciling with someone works out, but there will also be times when removing yourself from a conflict is the kindest thing you can do. Peace may mean drawing a boundary and saying, "I care about you. I forgive you, but the way you acted was not okay, and I have to walk away from this friendship." God has called us to chase after peace, not to fuel existing drama. No matter how hard the situation, our goal should always be to make sure we react to conflict in a way that honors God and shows others that we trust him to be our protector and defender.

God has called us to chase after peace, not to fuel existing drama.

Day 80

THE MYSTERY OF GRACE

2 CORINTHIANS 9:8

And God is able to make every grace overflow to you, so that in every way, always having everything you need, you may excel in every good work.

For most of my life, a huge wooden sign has hung in our living room with my mom's favorite quote from Anne Lamott. Every morning before school, I would read it while I ate my breakfast. At the time I didn't even realize it, but I memorized the quote. Those words now stand as a reminder of the ways God has worked in my life. The quote states: "I do not understand the mystery of grace—only that it meets us where we are and does not leave us where it found us."*

We use mercy and grace interchangeably so I once asked someone the difference between them. They explained that God's mercy spares us from something that we deserve. For example, Jesus took up our sin and died the death we deserve on the cross. Grace, on

* Anne Lamott, *Traveling Mercies: Some Thoughts on Faith* (Pantheon Books, 1999), 143.

the other hand, means that we are not only spared from what we deserve but then given freedom and joy above and beyond that.

It can be easy to sit back and wrestle with God about why we have to go through something difficult. Adversity is the worst. I mean, there have been times in my life where I have really had to have a chat with God about all of the character development he put me through because I feel like my character has been developed enough.

And clearly he doesn't agree with me, which just feels rude.

We can forget that it is in these very times when we are struggling that God's grace meets us. He will give us more than we can handle on our own, and it will feel hard, but thank God we have his grace to push us to that finish line. Not only will it help us walk through the hard times, but we will receive more than we can imagine on the other side. His grace blesses us and he delights in our joy and excitement over those blessings.

God's infinite grace meets us in the middle of our overwhelming struggles—the lost friend group, the breakup, the failed test—and does not leave us there. He picks us up in the places where we can't go any further on our own and gives us strength we didn't even know we had. Grace comes from a dependence on God and surrendering your struggles to him, knowing he will not let you down and will not leave you where you are.

God's infinite grace meets us in the middle of our overwhelming struggles and does not leave us there.

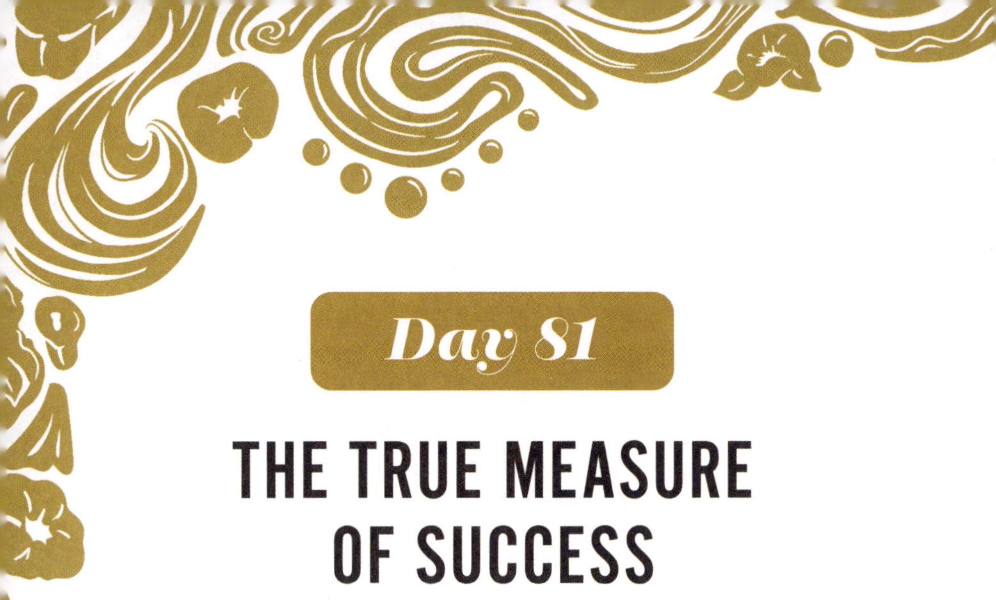

Day 81

THE TRUE MEASURE OF SUCCESS

1 SAMUEL 16:7

Humans do not see what the Lord sees, for humans see what is visible, but the Lord sees the heart.

Our God is a God of relationships. He cares more about relationships and people than anything else, and I think we can forget that a huge part of his purpose for us is found in the people he puts in our lives.

I tend to be an overachiever at times. I always want to succeed and keep climbing my way to the top, whether that's through sports, grades, or jobs. We say we want to succeed in order to glorify God, but the question is, how exactly does our success glorify him?

Ultimately, real success is found in the people we interact with and influence along the way. What glorifies God is the love and faith his people bring to a hurting world, not getting an A on a test or making the varsity team. God places us in positions to love people. Our worldly success can be used to draw people in so we can tell them about Jesus and how our relationship with him is the real, lasting thing that defines us.

Life is not about just climbing the ladder of success that the world tries to tell us is the thing that will satisfy our soul. It's about loving and caring for those around us. I see so many people in college trying to "network" and meet all of the "right" people in order to get a better job or to use them as a stepping stone for their success, and I can't help but think that is not how it's supposed to be. We should never look at other people and think, "How can they serve me?" We should look at those around us and think about how we can get to know them, pray for them, and support them. The only real way to be effective is to have true concern for the people around us.

Think about Jesus choosing his disciples. He didn't look for the most qualified rabbis or highest-ranking Jews within society; he chose people who had heart. He chose random outcasts who were capable of great things and just didn't realize it yet. He also didn't broadcast his qualifications. I mean, imagine if he just walked up to people, shook their hand, and said, "Nice to meet you, I'm the Son of God." He loved, he healed, and he was intentional with each person he met, and that led to those around him believing he truly was the Savior. His encouragement, prayer, and love for people led those disciples into their full potential in helping the kingdom of God and that love changed the world forever. How different would life look if we took that same approach with people around us?

What glorifies God is the love and faith his people bring to a hurting world.

Day 82

YOU WON'T FEEL THIS WAY FOREVER

JEREMIAH 30:19

Thanksgivings will pour out of the windows;
laughter will spill through the doors.
Things will get better and better.
Depression days are over. (MSG)

My senior year of high school was not my favorite time in my life. There was really nothing as depressing as watching all the fun things I thought that year would include get lost to a pandemic. There was no homecoming dance or parade, there was no bonfire, and there wasn't a prom. And, while I had friends, I didn't really have anyone that I felt safe with or like I could trust. When I look back at that time, I remember an overall feeling of loneliness and isolation that seemed like it would last forever.

Maybe you're in a similar place right now. Maybe you're going through a breakup, struggling to find friends, or fighting with your parents. I remember days when I wished I could just stay in bed. There are going to be seasons of life that are really tough. We are going to get our hearts broken, we are going to have friends betray our trust, and we are going to face situations that make us feel alone at times.

So what's the good news? No matter what you are going through, you have a God who loves you and sees every tear you've cried. And here are two things I've learned about hard times:

1. God will use every bit of what you are going through for good.
2. The struggle you're going through won't last forever, and better days are ahead.

You have an enemy who wants to keep you discouraged by making you believe that things won't ever get better. He wants to keep you feeling defeated because that is the quickest way to destroy what God has ahead for you. There is no heartbreak, no friend drama, no disappointment that God can't use in your life if you keep seeking him.

As hard as my senior year was, I can look back now and see all the ways that God was using those very things to prepare me for what he had ahead. It made me ready for college in a way I might not have been ready if I had loved every bit of high school. It made me treasure the friendships I have now because I know what it feels like to not have close friends. And those lonely weekends at home with my parents helped me grow closer to them in a way I might not have if I'd been out with friends all the time.

God is using the battles you face today to help you grow stronger for all that he has ahead. Trust him and know you won't feel this way forever.

The struggle you're going through won't last forever, and better days are ahead.

Day 83

COUNT ON HIM

MICAH 7:7

But me, I'm not giving up.
I'm sticking around to see what God will do.
I'm waiting for God to make things right.
I'm counting on God to listen to me. (*MSG*)

I love this verse in Micah. It just makes me happy. In my mind, I get this image of an extremely headstrong person holding out for hope and not leaving until they get it. Maybe they've been wronged or they lost something that really hurt and it's been a long journey. People are telling them it's time to move on or give up, and they are standing there with their arms crossed, saying, "Absolutely not. I know what my God promised, and he's going to deliver on that promise." It describes a stubborn, competitive nature, and I respect it so much. I believe God loves to see us like this.

God isn't afraid of a challenge. He wants us to call him out and believe in his power just like this verse describes. He wants us to count on him and to have full faith that he can and will make things right. He wants us to draw that line in the sand, shout out to him, and count on the fact that he's going to listen.

In a way, it almost feels like righteous anger. Like the enemy is working so hard to discourage us in the hard times and wants us so badly to believe the lie that God is going to leave us like this and then we get mad. This verse is a declaration that we aren't going to give the enemy a single inch in our life.

In the movie *School of Rock*, Jack Black's character tells his elementary school students about "the man" and how in life "the man" always tries to get you down. "The man" is the one with authority, who won't let you do something fun. "The man" gives you that failing grade or tells you all of the things you aren't capable of doing.

Throughout life there will be people who are going to tell you to give up or lose faith. Sometimes it will be the voice inside your own head telling you that. But God wants us to keep pushing and keep going. We have to cast out the lies and the critical voices that run through our head. Get rid of the doubt and say, "I'm not walking out now. So help me, I'm going to stick around to see God make this right." And then watch what he does.

God isn't afraid of a challenge. He wants us to call him out and believe in his power.

THE WEEKLY RECAP

Five Truths to Remember:

1. God's wisdom is deeper than ours, so we should hold our plans with an open hand.
2. We can't control what others may say or do to us, but God is always with us, even when we are in the middle of a hurtful situation.
3. Grace comes from a dependence on God and from surrendering our struggles to him, knowing he will not let us down and will not leave us where we are.
4. The struggle we are going through won't last forever, and better days are ahead.
5. God isn't afraid of a challenge. He wants us to call him out and believe in his power.

Three Questions to Ask:

1. What plans for your life are you holding on to a little too tightly?

2. When were you in a situation that seemed hopeless or like things would never get better?

3. Do you believe that God has the power to change your circumstances and use even the hard things in your life for good?

Day 85

GOD'S BEST

JOB 42:2–3

I know that you can do anything
and no plan of yours can be thwarted. . . .
Surely I spoke about things I did not understand,
things too wondrous for me to know.

C. S. Lewis once said, "We are not necessarily doubting that God will do the best for us; we are wondering how painful the best will turn out to be."*

Walking in faith is not necessarily easy. It requires trusting that God sees the bigger picture. It means there will be times God tells us no or redirects us. It can be frustrating to keep holding out for the best because there are other "good" things we could settle for, even if those things aren't exactly what God has for us.

God's redirection or his no reminds me of a parent not letting a little kid run into the street. The kid just wants to play and doesn't understand why his dad won't let him run around, but the dad

*C. S. Lewis, letter to Peter Bide, April 29, 1959, in *Letters of C. S. Lewis*, ed. W. H. Lewis and Walter Hooper (HarperOne, 2017), 610.

understands the danger and isn't going to allow it just because his kid is upset. He knows an upset kid is better than an injured one, and he knows that he is acting out of love for his child.

God handles us the same way. His redirection can be really frustrating and his no can feel unfair, especially when there is something we really, really want. I cannot tell you how many times I have told God my plan and watched him do something totally different. But, without a doubt, it's because he sees a lot more than us.

Wanting God's best means full surrender to his ways, as mysterious as they usually seem. We must trust that God truly wants to see us full of joy and wants to bless us beyond our dreams. But seeing that come to fruition requires hard work, dedication, faith, and sacrifice. We have to quit trying to control our own happiness and the outcome of every situation we face and, instead, leave it to God. His best often means letting go of the thing we hold on to so tight and trusting that what is meant for us will not pass us by.

God truly wants to see us full of joy and wants to bless us beyond our dreams.

Day 86

A TIME TO BE FORGED

PHILIPPIANS 4:12–13

I know how to make do with little, and I know how to make do with a lot. In any and all circumstances I have learned the secret of being content—whether well fed or hungry, whether in abundance or in need. I am able to do all things through him who strengthens me.

We've all been told by someone that "singleness is a gift." Usually it's "Kyle," the youth pastor who got married at twenty, or "Trisha," who is in a secure relationship that'll end in marriage. It almost seems hypocritical of them to say this when obviously they loved this "gift" so much they couldn't wait to leave it behind. Thanks for your input, Kyle, but I'm not interested in your feel-good clichés today.

Being single is not necessarily a gift, especially after having your heart broken. However, it is a tool that you can wield to forge yourself into something better and stronger. If you have the right perspective and use it correctly, it will most definitely become a gift. It's all about how you treat this season of life.

If you choose to sit idle in it and spend your time feeling sorry for yourself, then it's not going to be a gift. Think about it this way:

When talking about a biblical community or a relationship, a common phrase you hear is "iron sharpens iron." In a good, healthy relationship, you and another person will sharpen each other and make each other better.

But think about the process iron has already gone through before it becomes a blade. It was heated and cooled, hammered and forged, moved from fire to water in seconds, then back to the anvil to be hammered again. This process was repeated multiple times.

The process of becoming a useful, strong blade is a lot like singleness. Yes, a lot more goes into the preparation of a person, but at least one of those forging steps can be found in a season of being on your own with Christ. So, instead of looking at singleness as a season that you just have to endure, look at it as a tool the Lord has provided you with to make yourself better. This is a time to gain confidence in yourself, to be independent, and to rely on the Lord and the Lord alone to give you peace and contentment. Don't spend this time worrying about how to make yourself more dateable; instead, focus on letting God make you into the kind of person you hope to attract. If you are not content with yourself, then it's hard to be in a healthy, biblical relationship. To truly sharpen another person, you have to be forged in the fire first.

Focus on letting God make you into the kind of person you hope to attract.

Day 87

THE ULTIMATE LOVE STORY

EXODUS 34:6

The Lord passed in front of him and proclaimed:

The Lord—the Lord is a compassionate and gracious God, slow to anger and abounding in faithful love and truth.

I love a good love story. I like movies where the guy gets the girl and they live happily ever after. Give me the end of *Pride and Prejudice* all day long when Eizabeth Bennett tells Mr. Darcy, "You may only call me Mrs. Darcy . . . when you are completely, and perfectly, and incandescently happy."* It's perfection.

I can't remember a time when I didn't know about God and his love for me. But I didn't realize until I got old enough to study the Bible on my own that God's story is the ultimate love story. Sometimes we reduce God to a nice Bible verse that makes us feel better or treat him like a last resort when life is hard. The truth is he's the ultimate love of our life. He pursued us relentlessly, long before we were even created. God looked at you, with all your failures and struggles, and said, "That's her. That's the one I want."

* *Pride and Prejudice*, directed by Joe Wright (Universal Pictures, 2005), 2:01:34.

I sometimes catch myself thinking God is just like those who have hurt me or let me down . . . friends I trusted, family who were supposed to love and protect me. But the thing about God is he is holy. He cannot sin, let alone sin against you. He is trustworthy and his love for you is never-ending, unconditional, and always secure, even when everything around you feels uncertain.

When God passed by Moses on the mountain, he described himself as compassionate, gracious, slow to anger, abounding in faithfulness, maintaining love, forgiving wickedness, rebellion, and sin (see Exod. 34:6). And he hasn't changed. He is a constant source of strength, and he doesn't conform to us and our weakness. He is the same yesterday, today, and forever.

Whatever you are going through, whatever sin you are struggling with, whatever heartache you are currently trying to heal, always remember who God is in your life. He overflows with love for you, and he protects his love for you even when you mess up. He is full of compassion for every hard thing you face, and his forgiveness and mercy are beyond your wildest imagination or darkest day.

When God looks at you, he is "incandescently happy." He wants you to let go of anything that's keeping you from believing how much he loves you. And when you read his Word and understand his heart for you, you will know that he is and will always be the King of Kings, Prince of Peace, the first and the last. He is everything that you need and the greatest love story of your life.

God looked at you, with all your failures and struggles, and said, "That's her. That's the one I want."

Day 88

ON NOT BECOMING WELL-ADJUSTED

ROMANS 12:2

Don't become so well-adjusted to your culture that you fit into it without even thinking. Instead, fix your attention on God. You'll be changed from the inside out. (MSG)

I went to a public high school, and it was really hard to stand for what I knew was true when I was surrounded by so many voices that told me otherwise. I remember one time when my science teacher looked right at me and asked, "How do you even believe it was possible to fit all those animals on the ark?" Honestly, it's a valid question and one that can be answered only by faith in God's ability to do what seems impossible.

We live in a culture that lacks faith and doesn't really want to hear any truth that doesn't serve our purpose or fit whatever narrative we choose to believe. It can be so easy to start to compromise our beliefs and our values before we even realize what's happening. We've been told that tolerance is a virtue, but the reality is that isn't true if what we are tolerating is contrary to what God says.

Social media doesn't help because we are inundated with images and voices that normalize things that don't honor God and who he has created us to be. And, listen, I like to scroll mindlessly on Instagram as much as anyone because there are some treasures to be found, but we also have to be mindful of what we are allowing ourselves to consume, especially if those things cause us to justify acting in a certain way or believing things that pull us away from God.

Ask him to show you if you are just going along with whatever the loudest voices tell you instead of following his lead. Don't let the world tell you that you are defined by your position on the team, the status of your relationship, or how good your grades are. Don't mindlessly follow a group of friends into doing things you know aren't right just so you can fit in. Going against the cultural norms will never be the easiest path, but God will always give you the strength you need to stand strong in your faith and speak out for what is good and true. Don't compromise who he has called you to be because, somewhere along the way, he has created the right opportunity, the right group of friends, and the right situation just for you. Nothing will light up your soul like leaning into who he is and what he has planned for your life. Don't conform to what is right in front of you and miss out on all that lies ahead.

Don't conform to what is right in front of you and miss out on all that lies ahead.

Day 89

LOOKING BACK

ECCLESIASTES 7:10

Don't say, "Why were the former days better than these?" since it is not wise of you to ask this.

With TV, movies, and social media, we live in a time when we can put rose-colored lenses over anything we want. We can make a quick reel with some good music and completely distort the reality of the situation. But I think it's easy for us to do that same thing in our minds. We can be especially guilty of this when we look back at the past. It's super easy to look back fondly at all of the good and maybe just skim over some of the not so good. We romanticize what we had because it was known and felt comfortable versus what the unknown future might hold. When we look ahead, we only see all the "what ifs," and that can be kind of scary.

In the Bible, Lot's wife famously decided to look back on what they had moved on from. God had spared Lot's family from his wrath and the destruction of their city. His only command, as they fled and moved on to what was next, was that they not look back at their former city. Lot's wife disobeyed, then became a pillar of salt. I think

this serves as a reminder to us that when God is delivering us from the past, the only way to truly step into the future is to not look back. That can be tricky, though, because for our future, there's no montage with good music playing. We have no clue what it's going to look like.

Ancient Latin mapmakers had a saying for unknown and uncharted waters. It was *hic sunt dracones* or "here be dragons." The unknown was represented as an intimidating, untamed beast because the unknown is scary. This is why it's so tempting to look back because the future can seem like a dragon. But what we have to remember is that God has gone before us and has seen all that is to come. He will be with us as we take every step forward.

The best thing we can do with that knowledge is to trust in him and follow where he leads. It's normal to want to look back, but stepping into the plan God has for you means looking ahead, focusing your eyes on his unwavering love, and having faith that you will never be alone in your journey. Don't miss all that he has for you by spending time looking back at what used to be. The best montage of your life may be right around the corner.

When God is delivering us from the past, the only way to truly step into the future is to not look back.

Day 90

FRIENDS THAT HOLD YOUR ARMS UP

EXODUS 17:12

Then Aaron and Hur supported his hands, one on one side and one on the other so that his hands remained steady until the sun went down.

One of the reasons I was asked to write this book was because my publisher had heard about my experience dealing with friend drama and mean girl issues. This was really the biggest battle I faced during those high school years, and at the time it was truly awful. But time has given me perspective on the good ways those difficult situations shaped me. It gave me strength, resilience, and grit that I have needed as life continued and other challenges came my way. I've also learned how much it means to have loyal, true friends and what it means to be a loyal, true friend myself.

In Exodus 17, the Amalekites show up and attack the Israelites. Moses orders Joshua to fight them and then Moses, Aaron, and Hur go to the top of the hill to oversee the battle. As long as Moses held up his hands, the Israelites were winning the battle. Any time he

lowered his hands, they began to lose. The problem was Moses's arms got tired. Maybe Moses shouldn't have skipped arm day at the gym.

Aaron and Hur saw what was happening and they found a way to help Moses not have to do this all on his own strength. They found a stone for him to sit on, and then they got on either side of him and helped him hold up his hands when he was too tired to do it alone. Like Moses, get some friends who will help you fight the battles you will face.

Friendships are going to change. Some people will be in your life for only a season. Some friends will turn their back on you for reasons you may never understand, whether it's out of jealousy, insecurity, or moving on to another group with different interests. This is just part of life.

But I've learned that there will also be friends who are committed to you no matter what comes your way. They will have your back, listen to you vent after a hard day, stand up for you, and be loyal. They will hold your hands up and tell you to pick your head up during your darkest, hardest season. These are the kind of friends to look for and to ask God to bring into your life. And the best way to find these kinds of friends is to be that kind of friend. This is the kind of love and loyalty that will carry you the rest of your life.

Like Moses, get some friends who will help you fight the battles you will face.

THE WEEKLY RECAP

Five Truths to Remember:

1. Even when we can't see God working, he is doing more than we know.
2. In a healthy relationship, we will sharpen each other and make each other better.
3. God is full of compassion for every hard thing we face, and his forgiveness and mercy are beyond our wildest imagination or darkest days.
4. God will always give us the strength we need to stand strong in our faith and speak out for what is good and true.
5. Good friends have each other's backs, listen to each other vent after a hard day, and stand up for each other.

Three Questions to Ask:

1. What are some places in my life where I need to trust that God is working?

2. Do I have healthy relationships where I am encouraging others to be who God has created them to be and being encouraged myself?

3. How can I work on being a better friend to those around me?

Day 92

SHIFT IN PERSPECTIVE

EZEKIEL 37:3

Then he said to me, "Son of man, can these bones live?"

I replied, "Lord God, only you know."

Before God does a big work in our lives, I believe he likes to get us into a place of complete surrender. Almost to a place where it's a little comical how many doors are closing. Recently I've been in this place. So many things are working out differently than I thought that the only explanation is that God is redirecting me from various paths I desired. I'm not going to lie, it's definitely been a little frustrating and I'm getting a little weary, but I just have to trust him until it makes sense.

It's nice knowing that this is such a normal feeling. We see examples of it throughout Scripture. One of my favorite moments like this is when God places Ezekiel in the valley of dry bones. He shows Ezekiel the destruction and desolation of this place, then asks, "Can these bones live?"

Ezekiel responds, "Lord God, only you know." I always imagine him kind of shaking his head, a little breathless, maybe even laughing a bit

at the absurdity of the question. Have you ever been asked something that you had absolutely no idea about and thought, *Why on earth are you asking me?* Or am I the only one?

Life can look like a complete mess with dry bones everywhere, but we can sit back, trusting that only God knows what's next.

During uncertain times in our life, we won't know what each day will bring and, if you're a planner like me, that may fill you with existential dread. But I think we have to shift our perspectives and become like the characters Larry and Teddy in *Night at the Museum*.

Larry: I have no idea what I'm going to do tomorrow.

Teddy: How exciting.*

I love this perspective, and I believe it's how we have to live as well. Only God knows what's going to happen next. So instead of being afraid of what may come, let's embrace the unknown. What if we look at what only God knows with excitement and anticipation instead of worry or pessimism?

Instead of being afraid of what may come, let's embrace the unknown.

---

* *Night at the Museum*, directed by Shawn Levy (20th Century Fox, 2006), 1:25:35.

Day 93

LETTING GO AND BEING STILL

PSALM 46:10

Be still, and know that I am God. (NIV)

One day during high school, I went over to a friend's house to hang out. We went into the kitchen to grab some food and were headed back to her bedroom when her brother decided it was a good idea to jump out and scare us. My friend immediately dropped her food and screamed, but I stood my ground and hit him. I didn't mean to do it. It was an involuntary response. He looked at me and said, "Dang, you're a fighter."

'Tis true. I am a fighter. People sometimes talk about having a fight-or-flight response, and I have proven time and time again that my gut instinct is to scream and then accidentally hit someone. Yeah, my friends don't like to jump out and scare me anymore.

This is why it can be hard for me to "be still." I want to form a strategy, come up with a solution, dig deep, and power through whatever comes my way. I don't want to seem vulnerable or weak.

But God keeps reminding me of these words in Psalm 46. When I looked up this verse, I saw that "be still" is actually the word *rapha* in Hebrew, which means to let go or to release something. In other words, what God is really saying here is that we need to surrender and trust him with the battles in front of us.

So what does that look like? When you think of surrendering during a battle, you may picture someone waving a white flag and dropping their weapon. But it really means letting go of pride, fear, and all the ways we try to protect ourselves.

True surrender looks like letting go of the way we thought things should look or the dreams we've held on to so tightly and, instead, trusting that God is always going to do something better. It's in this letting go that we get to know his heart for us better than we did before. What would your life look like and how could your faith grow if you let go of trying to fight every battle you face by yourself and trusted God to fight for you?

God's strength comes through our weaknesses and our vulnerability. We will find rest in him when we realize he is our protector and provider. When we realize he is everything we need, we gain the freedom to surrender our hopes, dreams, and desires to him. And it will ultimately help us know him more than we did before.

When we realize God is everything we need, we gain the freedom to surrender our hopes, dreams, and desires to him.

Day 94

SOMETHING OUT OF NOTHING

ROMANS 4:17

As it is written: I have made you the father of many nations—in the presence of the God in whom he believed, the one who gives life to the dead and calls things into existence that do not exist.

Sometimes we can forget how powerful the God we serve really is. We can read the Bible and all these wild stories about the miracles he performed or the ridiculous circumstances he brought people through but applying it to our mundane day-to-day lives can be a little difficult. I mean, it's hard to think about a God who can raise men from the dead dwelling in a grocery store or even in a classroom. For some reason, that just doesn't sound as poetic.

Realizing that God works in us and through us can also be hard to comprehend and embrace as reality. "God, here I am, and I need help on this math exam" doesn't seem as important a request as parting the Red Sea to save the Israelite people. But the wild thing is that we do have that same God dwelling in our hearts

and working through us, and he wants to help us in every aspect of our lives.

The part of this verse that stands out to me is he "calls things into existence that do not exist." I know we think about things like God's ability to raise the dead back to life, but how often do we think about the reality that he can conjure something out of absolutely nothing and that those words mean that he has the power to create something in us that didn't exist before? Where you say you are weak, he sees strength. Where you see fear, he sees courage. Where you see brokenness, he sees healing. Where you see nothing, he sees something that is worth valuing, cherishing, and loving.

I think about the story of Gideon found in Judges 6. Gideon was the youngest son of one of the weakest families in the city. When God sent an angel of the Lord to him, Gideon hid behind a winepress out of fear. But God looked at him and called him a valiant warrior. Where a human would've seen a coward, God called a valiant warrior into existence. Gideon then delivered Israel from the Midianites.

Our value is not in what others see in us or even in what we see in ourselves; our value comes from a God who calls things into existence that never were. How powerful is that? At any moment our God can forge something new in us. He can use us in ways we never could've dreamed. The God we read about in the Bible is still active and moving in our everyday lives. We serve a God who does a new thing in us every day. We serve a God who loves us, cherishes us beyond what we could ever fathom, and sees greatness in us where we may see nothing.

Our value comes from a God who calls things into existence that never were.

Day 95

ON PRAYER AND A GRATEFUL HEART

1 THESSALONIANS 5:16–18

Rejoice always, pray constantly, give thanks in everything; for this is God's will for you in Christ Jesus.

I'm grateful for the blessings in my life, but slowing down and speaking out that gratitude has always been a little tricky for me. This is probably not great since gratitude and dependence on the Lord are crucial to our growth and faith.

It's easy to sit down and pray when times are tough because in the hard times we see exactly how much we need God. We often draw closer to God when we face adversity than when times are good because we get in the habit of treating God a bit like a genie to call on when we have a wish.

God wants to hear our desires, and he wants us to tell him what's going on, but one of the most powerful things we can do in the hard times is rejoice. Our emotions and feelings tend to reside wherever our mind is preoccupied. It's like whenever you're running and you

stare at something in the distance. Even if you don't mean to, you casually start running toward what you're focused on and away from the path you were following. When you focus on the struggle and on the hard moments, your feelings and thoughts will turn toward that and maybe even obsess over it a little bit.

However, if you focus on the good in your life and remember the blessings God has given you, your perspective will shift. There is wisdom in remembering what God has done because it helps us believe what he will do. That's why worship is so powerful. We sing out to God and remember his power, his splendor, and his provision.

Nehemiah 8:10 says, "The joy of the Lord is your strength." This is the truth. We have to choose joy in the rough times. We can be thankful for the small things and remember we serve a God who always has our best interest in mind. So rejoice and, as hard as it can be, take time to remember all the things you can be grateful for, and all the ways he has taken care of you, and believe him for what he will do in the future.

There is wisdom in remembering what God has done because it helps us believe what he will do.

Day 96

CUTTING OFF WHAT IS HURTING YOU

1 CORINTHIANS 15:33

Do not be deceived: "Bad company corrupts good morals."

I don't mean to brag, but I have a three-legged dog. I know, it's as amazing as it sounds.

Piper was born with four legs, but when she was about eight, she contracted a fungus in her front paw that couldn't be treated with medication. We took her to several doctors to find answers, but they all agreed the only cure would be to amputate her front leg. We weren't sure how losing a leg would affect her, but in the years since her surgery, it has been incredible to see her stay as active as she was before it happened. Our vet said the diseased paw had likely been causing her more pain than we realized. We had tried to avoid the amputation because it seemed so harsh, but the only way Piper was going to be able to heal was to cut off the source of the thing that was causing her pain.

This has made me think of friendships and relationships God ultimately had to remove from my life so that I could be healthy and

walk the way I am supposed to walk. Those amputations didn't feel great at the time, but I can see now how the people in my life he removed were bringing me down instead of lifting me up.

Maybe you are in this place right now. It can be hard to walk away from a friendship, even if it has become toxic. But you have to ask yourself—is this person drawing me closer to Christ? Are you having a positive impact on them or are they causing you to act in a way that you know doesn't align with God's will?

As my friends and I got older and gained more freedom to make our own decisions, I watched some of them make decisions I knew weren't right. Maybe you've heard an adult in your life say, "You are known by the company you keep," and maybe you've rolled your eyes like I have, but it's true. If you find yourself with friends who are making you do things you wouldn't normally do, or if you always have this uneasy feeling that they are talking about you behind your back, those aren't your friends. If you continually have to compromise what you know is right to fit in with a group, it might be time to walk away and find people who will love you for who you are and encourage you to be all that God is calling you to be.

Ask yourself—is this person drawing me closer to Christ?

Day 97

THE ULTIMATE TRAINER

PSALM 144:1–2

Blessed be the Lord, my rock
who trains my hands for battle
and my fingers for warfare.
He is my faithful love and my fortress,
my stronghold and my deliverer.
He is my shield, and I take refuge in him.

If I added up the hours I've spent training and practicing for soccer, the number would be somewhere around infinity. For years, all I wanted was to be the best player I could possibly be. I spent any free time juggling a soccer ball in my backyard, training with a strength and speed trainer, and practicing shooting goals to develop the muscle memory I would need to give myself the best chance to score in any game situation.

In his book *Outliers*, Malcolm Gladwell says that it takes ten thousand hours of intensive practice to truly become a master at something. But the research from that same study shows another important factor to becoming truly great at something—how good a student's teacher is at helping them learn a skill. The study showed that it's possible to be outperformed by someone who practiced less but had a teacher who showed them the most important things to focus on to improve their skills.*

Based on my experience with soccer coaches and trainers, I can say that this is so true. I had amazing coaches who really helped me develop as a player, and I had some not-so-great coaches who actually caused me not to play to the best of my ability because they wanted me to focus on things that didn't ultimately matter in a game situation.

This is why I love Psalm 144. David had to fight many battles in his life, and he knew that the victories he claimed were because of the teacher who trained him for battle. The strategies he learned, the way he knew to throw a stone, and any strength he had all came from God. He was the source of David's strength. God delivered him from every battle because David trusted in him to be his shield. He knew that he had a teacher he could rely on to deliver him from every battle.

It's the same way for us. We will face situations that are beyond our understanding or our abilities to defend ourselves. But we have the ultimate teacher who is always training us and equipping us for every hard time or disappointment that comes our way. Trust him to train you for the things you will deal with in life, knowing that he is going to help you focus on what really matters. We have the best teacher who is always just a "help me, please" away.

We have the ultimate teacher who is always training us and equipping us for every hard time or disappointment that comes our way.

---

* Jeffrey R. Young, "Researcher Behind '10,000-Hour Rule' Says Good Teaching Matters, Not Just Practice," EdSurge, May 5, 2020, https://www.edsurge.com/news/2020-05-05-researcher-behind-10-000-hour-rule-says-good-teaching-matters-not-just-practice.

THE WEEKLY RECAP

Five Truths to Remember:

1. Only God knows what's going to happen next, and instead of being afraid of what may come, we can choose to embrace it and trust him.
2. True surrender looks like letting go of the way we thought things should look or the dreams we've held on to so tightly and, instead, trusting that God is always going to do something better than what we thought we wanted.
3. Where we say we are weak, he sees strength. Where we say we are afraid, he sees courage. Where we see brokenness, he sees healing. Where we see nothing, he sees something that is worth valuing, cherishing, and loving.
4. Remembering what God has done in the past helps us believe in what he will do in the future.
5. We can trust God to train us for the things we will deal with in life, knowing that he is going to help us focus on what really matters and win the battles we face.

Three Questions to Ask:

1. What is God asking you to surrender to him and trust him with the outcome?

2. How have you seen God be faithful in other hard circumstances you have faced?

3. What are some ways you can train for the battles you are dealing with right now?

Day 99

FIGHTING OFF THE FLAMING ARROWS

EPHESIANS 6:16

In every situation take up the shield of faith with which you can extinguish all the flaming arrows of the evil one.

For my twenty-first birthday, I asked for a bow and arrows because I really wanted a new challenge. I was also perhaps influenced by Merida from *Brave*. Shooting an arrow for your own hand feels like a powerful skill. Archery requires discipline and precision, and it takes a lot of practice to become proficient.

Practicing my archery skills has made me think about this verse in Ephesians and "the flaming arrows of the evil one." After spending time shooting my bow, this feels like a more pointed attack of the enemy than I've ever realized before.

In our lives, we probably don't have an enemy shooting actual arrows at us, unless your life is a lot more eventful than mine. But we do have an enemy who is always looking to attack our every insecurity and vulnerability. Maybe some of your flaming arrows sound like this:

"You're not as pretty as other girls."
"Everyone is smarter than you."
"You are never going to have real friends."
"You'll never meet the man you want to spend the rest of your life with."
"No one will love you for you."
"God is so disappointed in you and the ways you keep messing up."

I'm guessing some of these things run through your head, keep you up at night, and make you feel like you will never measure up. This is a strategic attack from an enemy who is always looking for ways to keep you from walking in the incredible fullness of God's plan for you.

But here's the other thing I've learned as I've practiced with my bow: It doesn't take much to deflect an arrow from its target. With God we have an impenetrable shield of faith that can protect us from every arrow of doubt and destruction the enemy shoots our way. For every lie the enemy uses to try to take us down, we have the power to defeat it with the truth of who God says we are.

Goodness and mercy will follow you all the days of your life. (see Ps. 23:6)
You are loved. (see Ps. 103:11)
You are mine. (see Isa. 43:1–2)
Nothing can separate you from my love. (see Rom. 8:38–39)
You are chosen. (see Eph. 1:4–5)

Regardless of the attack you are facing right now, take up your shield of faith and fight back with the truth of how God sees you.

It doesn't take much to deflect an arrow from its target.

Day 100

A FAITHFUL STEP FORWARD

1 SAMUEL 17:48

When the Philistine started forward to attack him, David ran quickly to the battle line to meet the Philistine.

We live in a broken world with broken people. It's not a matter of if you will face adversity, it's a matter of when. The whole takeaway of Christianity is a hope for something greater. Greater than pain, sadness, hurt, and loss. This hope is what we hold on to in the good and in the bad we will face. God can turn any of the darkness in this world into his light, and he's going to use us to do it.

Look back at David and Goliath. The giant David had to face was the very stepping stone he needed to become king. Without Goliath, David might have stayed in the field tending to sheep. I think sometimes we look at adversity and we let it define us, but the reality is that the defining aspect of adversity is how we handle it. Do we run toward the battle, stone in hand, knowing our God will deliver us like he delivered David? Do we remember the lions and bears God has delivered us from as we face our giants?

David knew God before he faced Goliath, but he saw God and his power in a new way after the battle. David didn't know it would lead to him becoming king; all he did in that moment was take a faithful step forward.

But God saw the strength there and he saw the fire in David. He walked David through that battle because he was forging something greater in him and knew that David was his guy. He was building a warrior who would deliver his nation. Why do we think God won't go through our battles with us?

While we might not ever have to face a giant, we will face smaller battles and trials. God desires to forge a strength in us, one that we might not know exists yet. When we face trials and battles, God sees a strength in us that we don't even see in ourselves. So don't let the hard times define you. Instead, be defined by the strength God displays in you and the way you prevail in the face of adversity. This world is in desperate need of strong women. It needs leaders, wives, mothers, and daughters who will run to battle and deliver their people. You are that woman, and you are that leader. Never underestimate the power of God and how he will use you to change the world around you.

Be defined by the strength God displays in you and the way you prevail in the face of adversity.

A Note from Melanie

My hope and prayer is that God has met you at every turn as you've read Caroline's words of hope and encouragement over the last 100 days. Before you close these pages, I want to challenge you with this: Don't let what God has planted in your heart during this season be forgotten just because you are finished with this book. The challenge for you now is to keep becoming the woman God is calling you to be. It will not always be easy, it will not always be fun, and it won't always feel good. I'm sorry, but I have to be honest. I've lived long enough to know that there are going to be hard seasons ahead. The key is to never lose your grip on who Jesus is and all the ways he will give you the strength and hope you need to get through whatever hard times come.

Let him be the hope that carries you through a dark night, the love that brings contentment and peace when you feel alone, and the guiding light that will always lead you to safety amid life's storms.

I also encourage you to go back and highlight the parts of this book that have meant the most to you. Go back and reread some of the statements or entries that stood out. Go back and write notes in the margins about what God taught you or showed you as you read. It's a great way to chart your journey and, one day, look back at all the prayers God answered. I can think of no better way to believe he will be faithful in your future than to remember where he was faithful in your past.

Finally, know that Caroline and I are praying for you. We may not know you by name, but we have prayed for every girl who picks up this book and reads these words. That means you qualify. We love you, God loves you, and no matter what lions, bears, or giants you are facing, everything is going to be all right.

> May the God of hope fill you with all joy and peace as you trust in him, so that you may overflow with hope by the power of the Holy Spirit.
>
> Romans 15:13 (NIV)

Acknowledgments

Well, full transparency, if you had told me in 2023 that I would be writing a book my junior and senior year of college, I probably would've laughed and told you that writing is my mom's thing, not mine. Yet here I am a few years later, sitting down writing acknowledgments for my first book. There is only one reason this is happening, and it's because of the Lord himself. I sit here utterly humbled at the fact that God would entrust this devotional to me and that people actually want to read what I have to say.

First, I want to thank God for his sovereignty, his light, and his love. He is my Savior, my shepherd, and my shield. I never would've been able to do any of this without him. As I wrote this devotional, there were plenty of ups and downs, and he carried me the whole way. Job 23:10 states: "But He knows the way that I take [and He pays attention to it]. When He has tried me, I will come forth as [refined] gold [pure and luminous]" (AMP). Through his discipline and his love, this devotional has felt like my gold. I am beyond grateful for what God has instilled in me. This whole devotional is because of him.

Like I said above, I never really thought of writing or storytelling as one of my gifts, and I probably still wouldn't if it weren't for my agent Lisa Jackson and editor Andrea Doering. Thank y'all for taking a chance on a twenty-something-year-old and giving my voice a platform. I have become a better writer because of y'all, and this never would've been a reality for me if it wasn't for your belief in me.

Thank you, as well, to the editorial, marketing, sales, and publicity teams at Revell. You have helped me and my mom bring this vision to life and made it everything we hoped it could be. I want to specifically thank Robin for making me a better writer and for making this book the best it can be. Also, a special thanks to the artists and design team on the cover art. It truly made me giddy the first time I saw it.

I want to also say thank you to all the incredible older women in my life. God has thoroughly blessed me with some of the toughest, coolest women to learn from. Jennifer Ann, Jean Marie, Sarah Chilton, and Stephanie, thank you for showing me that it's okay to be completely authentic in myself and that having a spicier personality is nothing to apologize for. Retha and Sophie, thank you for always being there for my mom and, by proxy, me as well. I'm so grateful for your support and encouragement.

Lyndi, I would not have made it through spring semester of my junior year without you. You have been my ride or die, and learning how to be a real adult with you has been such a blessing. You know me better than I know myself sometimes, and when I've had a bad day, you always find a way to make it better. I'm so grateful that we became fast friends on a ski trip freshman year.

There are always lots of jokes about girls that end up with their dad's personality, but I have to say I wouldn't want it any other way. I couldn't be prouder when someone calls me a "mini Perry." Dad, thank you for your constant support, honesty, and wisdom. You have made me into a fighter and instilled a grit and resilience in me that I will forever be grateful for. You have showed me what a man of God looks like and have been my rock all along.

Mom, none of this would be remotely possible without you. You are my role model, and I'm so proud to be your daughter. No matter what, you have shown me unwavering support, whether it was me wanting to play the flute in sixth grade (knowing this would be a catastrophe) or taking a leap of faith and following in your footsteps. The way you have loved and sacrificed for me is something that I can only aspire to do for my own children one day. Thank you for helping me write this devotional and for making me better along the way.

About the Authors

CAROLINE SHANKLE is an animal science major at Texas A&M University. She graduates in May 2025 and is planning to pursue a master's degree. In addition, she hopes to write more books and speak to young women about the battles they face. She wrote this book on Fruity Pebbles coffee and a prayer. She enjoys long walks on the beach, along with archery. She loves hunting, anything outdoors, reading great fiction books, and spending time with her friends. She also would like to know how she's already gotten jury duty three times in four years of living in College Station, but that's an issue for another day. Thanks, and gig 'em.

Connect with Caroline:

 **@CarolineShankle**

MELANIE SHANKLE is the *New York Times* bestselling author of *Sparkly Green Earrings, The Antelope in the Living Room, Nobody's Cuter Than You,* and *Here Be Dragons*. She speaks at events nationwide and cohosts the wildly popular podcast *The Big Boo Cast*. She is a graduate of Texas A&M who loves writing, checking to see what's on sale at Anthropologie, and looking for the bright side in every situation. Most of all, she loves being the mother of Caroline and the wife of her husband, Perry.

Connect with Melanie:

 @MelanieShankle

A Note from the Publisher

Dear Reader,

Thank you for selecting a Revell book! We're so happy to be part of your life through this work.

Revell's mission is to publish books that offer hope and help for meeting life's challenges, and that bring comfort and inspiration. We know that the right words at the right time can make all the difference; it is our goal with every title to provide just the words you need.

We believe in building lasting relationships with readers, and we'd love to get to know you better. If you have any feedback, questions, or just want to chat about your experience reading this book, please email us directly at publisher@revellbooks.com. Your insights are incredibly important to us, and it would be our pleasure to hear how we can better serve you.

We look forward to hearing from you and having the chance to enhance your experience with Revell Books.

The Publishing Team at Revell Books
A Division of Baker Publishing Group
publisher@revellbooks.com

Notes

Notes

Notes

Notes

Notes

Notes